A PRACTICAL GUIDE TO PLAY IN EDUCATION

The benefits of play for children's learning are well-documented and well-researched. The evidence for its positive impact on brain development, social interactions, emotional wellbeing, and motor skills is widespread. So, why should this practice stop after the early years?

A Practical Guide to Play in Education encourages teachers to reflect on their practice and consider how a play-based approach may enhance their teaching. It provides realistic, accessible ideas and resources to incorporate into practice while giving evidence to back up this approach.

Divided into three clear sections, readers are guided through:

- An introduction to play in education, including theory, benefits, and potential challenges.
- Putting it into practice, such as setting up the classroom, resources for play, and adopting a playful ethos in a realistic and accessible way.
- Lesson plans in a variety of subjects, spanning from numeracy, to literacy, to health and wellbeing.

This unique and practical book highlights the importance of play in helping children develop skills to support their future and demonstrates how this approach can be seamlessly integrated into teaching styles across primary and early secondary.

Michelle Simpson has worked with children for almost 30 years, with over half of that time as a teacher specialising in supporting learners and inclusion. Still in the classroom, she enjoys developing new pedagogical approaches which enhance inclusion, engagement, and overall enjoyment of learning and teaching.

A PRACTICAL GUIDE TO PLAY IN EDUCATION

Primary School and Beyond

Michelle Simpson

LONDON AND NEW YORK

Designed cover image: Getty Images

First published 2025
by Routledge
4 Park Square, Milton Park, Abingdon, Oxon OX14 4RN

and by Routledge
605 Third Avenue, New York, NY 10158

Routledge is an imprint of the Taylor & Francis Group, an informa business

© 2025 Michelle Simpson

The right of Michelle Simpson to be identified as author of this work has been asserted in accordance with sections 77 and 78 of the Copyright, Designs and Patents Act 1988.

All rights reserved. No part of this book may be reprinted or reproduced or utilised in any form or by any electronic, mechanical, or other means, now known or hereafter invented, including photocopying and recording, or in any information storage or retrieval system, without permission in writing from the publishers.

Trademark notice: Product or corporate names may be trademarks or registered trademarks, and are used only for identification and explanation without intent to infringe.

British Library Cataloguing-in-Publication Data
A catalogue record for this book is available from the British Library

ISBN: 978-1-032-78182-2 (hbk)
ISBN: 978-1-032-78183-9 (pbk)
ISBN: 978-1-003-48660-2 (ebk)

DOI: 10.4324/9781003486602

Typeset in Interstate
by Apex CoVantage, LLC

CONTENTS

Introduction — 1

SECTION 1 A Play-Based Pedagogy — 3

1 What is Play? — 5

2 The Benefits of a Play-Based Approach — 12

3 Play in the Early Years and Beyond — 19

4 Putting the Principles into Action — 27

5 Barriers and Solutions — 32

6 Record Keeping — 38

SECTION 2 Putting it into Practice — 45

7 Setting the Scene — 47

8 Resources — 52

9 Creating a Playful Ethos — 57

SECTION 3 Practical Lesson Ideas — 67

10 Numeracy and Mathematics — 69

11 Literacy — 83

12 STEAM — 95

13 Health and Wellbeing — 107

14	**Other Subject Areas**	117
15	**Project-Based Learning**	124
16	**Continuous Provision**	130
17	**Concluding Thoughts**	140

Useful Websites and Links — 142
Appendix A: APDR and PDSA — 144
Appendix B: Timetable — 146
Appendix C: Construction Materials — 147
Index — 149

Introduction

Some people are destined to be teachers from a young age. I'm not sure I am necessarily one of them.

After studying Physiology and Sports Science and then successfully gaining my MSc in Sports Studies, I coached for a few years before realising that working with children was something I enjoyed. But I wanted to do something more general than sport, so teacher training followed and now, almost 20 years later, I am still training, studying, and learning new ways to develop my practice. I am currently teaching in a primary school in the northeast of Scotland, and I regularly seek to try out and develop new ways to improve my pedagogy. The idea of a play-based approach for older learners is relatively new. This book contains many of the activities that have proven successful in my classroom, and I have tried out every one of them. It is a welcome quest for me to develop new ways to improve a play-based or contextual pedagogy to make it suitably challenging for older learners.

A few years ago, I would have scoffed at the notion of Play in the upper stages. Isn't play more for younger children? They won't learn anything; they'll just choose to play rather than learn. How on earth would I find the time for that?!

Now, however, following an enforced lockdown, teaching a class from my spare room, and some research into alternative teaching and learning styles and practices, I have a new perspective. Play is a concept, an approach to learning that, if used effectively, can benefit learners of all ages. Children of any age don't choose to play rather than learn; they learn as they play. It's up to us as educators to facilitate this in a way that challenges and maximises learning opportunities.

This book is an account of my journey into Play in the Upper Stages and how I have learned to find a balance between the traditional methods of teaching and introducing a playful pedagogy to my more senior classes. It also shares some examples of how I have implemented a 'play' approach while keeping attainment and progress at the forefront of my practice as well as a whole raft of lesson ideas to help you on your own play journey.

Acronyms used in this book:

STEAM   Science, Technology, Engineering, Arts, Mathematics
BODMAS   Brackets, Order, Division, Multiplying, Addition, Subtraction

PEDMAS	Parenthesis, Exponents, Division, Multiplication, Addition, Subtraction
HMIe	His Majesty's Inspectorate of Education (Scotland)
APDR	Assess, Plan, Do, Review
PDSA	Plan, Do, Study, Act

SECTION 1
A Play-Based Pedagogy

1 What is Play?

Play is not just something fun that children enjoy doing; it is their right. It features in the United Nations Convention on the Rights of the Child in Article 31 if you would like to look it up (UNICEF, 2022). The right for all children to have rest and leisure, to engage in play and recreational activities and to participate in cultural life and the arts. It is a vital component of a child's development, and it happens to be fun. During play, cognitive skills, social skills, emotional development, impulse control, physical motor skills, mental health, and so much more are all being acquired, setting the foundations for the future.

Play is widely accepted in educational literature as a tricky concept to define. Finding an agreed-upon definition for play is an elusive task. It can mean different things to different people. Having read through a variety of definitions, I am not about to present a concrete definition of play, but a quick compilation of some of the definitions includes:

- Done for its own sake
- Voluntary
- Improvised
- Free from time constraints
- No adult involvement
- Flexible
- Limitless
- Child-led
- Fun
- Engaging
- Desire to continue
- Enjoyable
- Chosen
- Infinite

One concept agreed by most is that play is a process; it is not one singular activity. It is voluntary, and it is child-led. There are some key elements that need to be present for an activity to be considered play. The core themes in all of the definitions I have found can be summarised into some main principles of play:

- It is freely chosen
- It is personally directed

- It is intrinsically motivated
- It is enjoyable and engaging

(Danniels and Pyle, 2018; Fleer, 2021; Ginsburg et al., 2007; Gray, 2009; McKendrick, 2019; Peterson, 2020; Scottish Government, 2013; Welsh Assembly Government, 2002).

When I refer to 'play' throughout this book, I will be referring to activities that embody these principles.

Play is integrated into the early years in quite an established way, but these elements of play can easily be considered in the learning opportunities we provide for our older learners, too. We just might not call it play. We want our learners of all ages to be able to motivate themselves, to direct their own learning, to make good choices, and enjoy their learning, don't we?

Imagine a situation where you offer your class free choice following a non-negotiable textbook task, and some choose to continue with their textbook work. To most people, this does not look like the child is playing. Shouldn't play be more fun, more energetic, more entertaining? But if completing extra textbook questions is what a learner has chosen to do, without any adult intervention, they are personally driven and intrinsically motivated to complete it, then technically, it is play. And it has happened in my classroom!

Play opportunities can be provided for children in different ways. The three main levels of play are Free Play, Play-based Learning, and Playful Learning. The difference between the three boils down to the level of involvement from the adults.

So, what do these different levels of play look like?

Play or Free Play

Play is essentially what children do whenever they are left completely to their own devices. True play is entirely child-led with minimal or no adult involvement. There are no instructions or guidance, and children are free to choose an activity that interests them. To many, this is the true meaning of play, and there is a train of thought that this is what should be happening in classrooms at all stages. Activities that fit into this category are free choice or free time, time where students are completely unrestricted in their choice of an activity that interests them using any materials that are available. The learning is unplanned and spontaneous. Learners are free to flow from one activity to another. Adults are not involved unless invited to participate, but only at the level requested by the child(ren).

Play-Based Learning or Guided Play

Play-based learning refers to a holistic approach to learning and development. Through play, children can learn valuable skills that support their social, physical, and cognitive development. Through engaging with others, objects, and symbols, children are supported to make sense of the world around them. In these situations, the opportunities are guided by adults – in this case, teachers – and there is more adult involvement than there is with true play. Learners still have some agency over their decisions and their actions. Activities in this category might include STEM challenges where a teacher presents a problem that the learners must find a solution to. The teacher does not instruct the class what they should do, and there are many opportunities for the play principles to be engaged, but the boundaries of the specific task prevent it from being free play. It is, nevertheless, a vital learning vehicle and one which allows teachers and educators to plan and direct the learning to a certain extent. It is a hybrid model of play pedagogy, a style of teaching that embraces play principles while keeping one eye on the curriculum and attainment results.

Playful Learning and Teaching or Playful Instruction

Playful learning and teaching are mainly adult-led. It involves teacher-initiated and supported tasks and activities that are considered more playful than traditional textbook or question-and-answer activities. Activities that might fit into this category include a class game of Multiplication Bingo or a game of basketball in the gym hall during PE. There is less opportunity for learners to take control of their learning or have any agency.

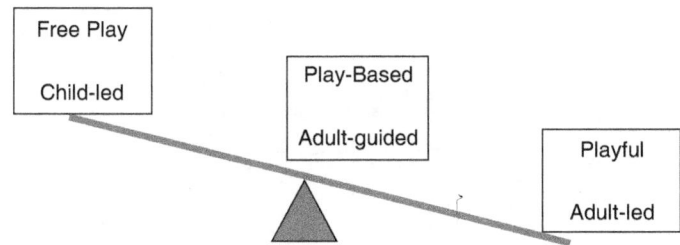

Adult involvement in play

There are also different types of play. Play can be creative, imaginative, exploratory, investigative, dramatic, physical, communicative, and many more types on top of that.

There are different categories of play as well. Gross motor skills are developed through whole-body movement and rough-and tumble-play, while fine motor skills are developed through more intricate activities involving Lego, threading, cutting, writing, balancing, and so on.

Different types of play can develop different skills and have different benefits.

Imaginative Play – role-playing and pretending help develop understanding of the world as well as potentially improve emotional resilience.

Creative Play – Making something new – drawing, writing, painting, building. Creative play allows learners to share and represent their ideas in their own ways.

Games with Rules – Children will inevitably bring rules and boundaries to their play: certain resources that are or aren't allowed, people who can or can't play. While this may look unkind to us from the outside, it gives them a sense of control; they are developing management skills, leadership skills, and perhaps some empathy as they see the reactions of their peers. For those not allowed to play, our instincts may be to intervene and support, but they are developing resilience and independence, managing their emotions, and learning how to deal with disappointment. But please make sure there are some fun alternatives nearby to avoid prolonged disappointment!

8 A Play-Based Pedagogy

Figure 1.1 Wooden Dolls

Social Play – playing with others helps nurture relationships and creates opportunities for conflict resolution, negotiating, compromising, co-operating, collaborating, turn-taking, and empathy. Play can be Solitary, Parallel, or Group Play, playing alone, beside others, or with others, but all contribute to the development of social interactions in the long run, as even solitary play helps children make sense of the world around them. Some children may choose to simply observe the play of others. This doesn't mean they can or won't play. It may be that their chosen activity is to watch and analyse their peers. It is all meaningful.

How has Play come into Play?

The position of play in the primary school has changed over the years. In the 1960s, play showed up as experiential learning, and this could be seen in all classes throughout primary school, all the way up to Year 6 or Primary 7. As time has gone on, play has been reserved more for the early years, while older pupils learned through topics and projects. National Curriculums and guidance saw a move towards more curricular planning and less project-based or themed learning. Play has remained an important part of learning in the early years, but until recently, older pupils have had their learning split into different subject areas and been taught in a step-by-step fashion in order to achieve a standard or benchmark. As seen recently, though, an interdisciplinary approach allows for a return to a more playful, project-based style of learning.

All nations in the UK have developed their educational policies towards a more play-based and developmentally appropriate approach to teaching and learning in the early years. This approach can also be known as an enriched curriculum and is designed to be responsive to the developmental stage of individual children. The aim of this approach was to remove the early experience of failure and promote a sense of self-competence and self-esteem. The teaching methods included more of an emphasis on play and activity-based learning rather than desk work in order to stimulate curiosity, creativity, social development, and engagement with learning (Walsh et al., 2010).

Now, play is finding its way into education policy in a more robust way. In Scotland, where I am based, play is located within educational policy through The Play Strategy, GIRFEC (Getting it Right for Every Child, the Scottish Government's commitment to providing all children, young people, and their families with the support they need) and the Curriculum for Excellence (CfE, Scottish Executive, 2004). Other national organisations have also promoted play, such as Play Scotland, Inspiring Scotland, The National Play Strategy for Scotland, and the Smart Play Network. I have looked wider, and there are also policies across the UK that support the development of Play (The Play Strategy, Play England, Play Wales, Wales: A Play Friendly Country and Play Matters; Playboard, Northern Ireland). The Right to Play is the right of all children worldwide. The development of play-based learning is an international movement that aligns educational policy with the science of how children learn. Briefly looking around the world, some examples of how organisations are advocating the benefits of play for our learners can be seen in Australia (Australian Children's Education and Care Quality Authority, Play Australia), Finland (Finnish National Agency for Education), India (Government of India, National Education Policy) and in the United States of America (AAP; Right to Play; US Play Coalition).

Policy supports the provision of play opportunities for older children as it rarely puts an age limit on the play provision for our learners. As mentioned previously, the principles of play are important for older learners, we just might refer to their application differently.

The Progress Review of Scotland's Play Strategy 2021 contains recommendations that include ensuring the inclusion of all children and young people (Scottish Government, 2021). Including all children and young people means offering them the same opportunities, so perhaps play should not be an educational experience reserved solely for those in the early years. This is particularly important considering the effects of the pandemic, in which lockdown periods deprived children of opportunities to play with their friends and develop social skills and relationships. Even beyond this, play helps learners develop their interactions with each other, build friendships, and develop other life skills that I will go into later. Providing these opportunities in school is crucial to truly meet the individual needs of every child.

It can be difficult to move towards change. Tradition tells us that children learn best when they are quiet and sitting still. Noise and movement do not equal an effective learning environment. Or so we have been led to believe. Teachers tend to want to separate things like movement and thinking. But do learners concentrate better if they are sitting? Or listen better if they are quiet and still? Recent research tells us that these concepts are integrated – movement can actually help learners listen and concentrate on what is being taught (Kleinjan,

2020). Conversation and physical activity can help learners process and make connections with the information being presented to them. If we keep this in mind, then sitting in chairs, standing at a desk, walking about, sitting on the floor, or even lying down, does it really matter where your learners complete their work if deep and meaningful learning is taking place and they are not distracting others?

So, after looking at what play entails, there are various ways it can be introduced into a learning environment. Once we look at some of the potential benefits of play, perhaps you will begin to see how it can fit into your own teaching style.

Take Away

Play is well established in the early years and forms an important part of the curriculum in many countries. It does not tend to be seen in classrooms beyond 7 or 8 years of age.

When applied correctly, however, play can be a fantastic vehicle for learning in learners beyond this age. And in the current climate, opportunities to play can provide vital benefits to the social and emotional wellbeing of our children.

Play is entirely child-led with minimal or no adult involvement. It may be the true meaning of play, but it is not the only way to play. Play-based learning is guided by adults – in our case, teachers – and there is more adult involvement than there is with true play. Playful learning and teaching are mainly adult-led and involve teacher-initiated and supported tasks and activities that are considered more playful than traditional textbook or question-and-answer activities.

There are benefits to all three approaches, and the most important thing to bear in mind is, which approach will best meet the needs of your learners.

References

Danniels, E., and Pyle, A. (2018). *Defining Play-Based Learning*. OISE University of Toronto, Canada. http://ceril.net/index.php/articulos?id=594

Fleer, M. (2021). *Play in the Early Years* (3rd Edition). Cambridge, UK: Cambridge University Press.

Ginsburg, K.R., American Academy of Pediatrics Committee on Communications, and American Academy of Pediatrics Committee on Psychosocial Aspects of Child and Family Health. (2007). The Importance of Play in Promoting Healthy Child Development and Maintaining Strong Parent-Child Bonds. *Pediatrics* 119(1): 182–191.

Gray, P. (2009). Play as a Foundation for Hunter-Gatherer Social Existence. *American Journal of Play* 1: 476–522 in Fleer, M. (2021). *Play in the Early Years* (3rd Edition). Cambridge, UK: Cambridge University Press.

Kleinjan, D. (2020). *Movement Matters: The Importance of Incorporating Movement in the Classroom [Literature Review]*. NWCommons. https://nwcommons.nwciowa.edu/cgi/viewcontent.cgi?article=1209&context=education_masters

McKendrick, J. (2019). Realising the Potential of Play in Scottish Education. *Scottish Educational Review* 51(2): 137–142.

Peterson, A. (2020). *Teach, Play, Learn! How to Create a Purposeful Play-Driven Classroom*. California: Dave Burgess Consulting.

Scottish Executive. (2004). *A Curriculum for Excellence*. Edinburgh: Scottish Executive.

Scottish Government. (2013). *Play Strategy for Scotland: Our Vision*. www.gov.scot/publications/play-strategy-scotland-vision/

Scottish Government. (2021). *Progress Review of Scotland's Play Strategy 2021: Play in a Covid-19 Context*. www.playscotland.org/wp-content/uploads/Play-Scotland-Play-Strategy-Review-Play-in-Covid-2021.pdf

UNICEF. (2022). www.unicef.org/child-rights-convention/convention-text-childrens-version#:~:text=The%20United%20Nations%20Convention%20on%20the%20Rights%20of,and%20they%20cannot%20be%20taken%20away%20from%20children

Walsh, G.M., McGuinness, C., Sproule, L., and Trew, K. (2010). Implementing a Play-Based and Developmentally Appropriate Curriculum in Northern Ireland Primary Schools: What Lessons Have We Learned? *An International Research Journal* 30(1): 53–66.

Welsh Assembly Government. (2002). *Play Policy*. https://play.wales/wp-content/uploads/2023/03/Play-Policy.pdf

2 The Benefits of a Play-Based Approach

What are the Benefits?

Children play from a young age, and the benefits of play-based learning for children in the younger years are well documented. A quick search of 'Play in the Early Years' will grant you as much reading material as you can handle.

Play for younger learners is widely accepted to be beneficial. We are who we are because of the experiences we have, not because of the facts we learn. Play allows opportunities for many of these experiences to be positive, safe, and supported. It helps young children develop a whole range of skills associated with their physical, mental, social, and emotional wellbeing. And there is no shortage of reading to back up this theory. I have done quite a bit of reading on the benefits of play, and it can be quite a lot to wade through, so let me save you the trouble and summarise some of my findings:

> Play provides an opportunity to develop social-emotional, cognitive, language, and self-regulation skills that contribute to the development of executive function. (Broadhead et al., 2010; Fleer, 2021; Palmer, 2019; Schlesinger et al., 2020; Sheridan, 2011; Walsh et al., 2010; Wood, 2013; Yogman et al., 2018 to give just some examples). It can develop problem-solving skills and critical thinking. Socially, it can aid with conflict resolution, negotiation, turn-taking, and sharing. The American Academy of Pediatrics (AAP) Clinical Reports on the importance of play (Ginsburg et al., 2007) and more recent research has illustrated the importance of play in nurturing relationships, developing executive functioning, enhancing social skills, building resilience, increasing independence and initiative as well as many other benefits (Dewar, 2023; Koepp et al., 2022; Nestor and Moser, 2018). Play that involves physical activity and movement supports the development of gross and fine motor skills, cardiovascular fitness, and the immune system (Lubans et al., 2010; Goldstein, 2012). Surely these are all benefits we want for our older learners just as much as our younger ones?

Play is essentially opportunity and experience – trying things out, exploring, investigating, and experimenting. It can offer older learners the challenge to enhance their learning in a contextual way if they are provided with the opportunity and materials to do so. Time to measure, write, research, or create, free from constraints, can undoubtedly help embed learning more securely.

Play can give learners the opportunity to try out scenarios and explore situations without the risk of real-life consequences. It is a safe way to explore, investigate, experiment, and try out theories – and if we provide these experiences in school, learners have the added benefit of having adults there who can help them make sense of their findings and extend their learning even further.

Play can be useful in supporting specific issues or trauma, but that would be an entirely different book. Reports do show that play could be vital in supporting children in understanding and recovering from the effects of major events (Riley and Jones, 2010; Young, 2021), and this might be worth keeping in mind should we think our learners need it, particularly following events such as the recent coronavirus pandemic.

Playful learning can enrich the learning experience of all learners, utilising the pupil-choice element of play, and giving them more responsibility for their own learning in an age and stage-appropriate way (Krechevsky et al., 2019). Play can be used to increase engagement, motivation, and enjoyment through fun learning opportunities. In my support for learning roles, I have used play to great effect to engage previously disengaged learners.

But can it have an impact on attainment? It has been linked with the development of language and literacy (Christie and Roskos, 2006), communication and concentration (Danniels and Pyle, 2018), and self-regulation (Zachariou and Whitebread, 2015), but what we're looking for is assessment data. These skills all contribute to progress in academic achievement, and the development of these skills and attributes does not stop as learners leave the early or infant stages of their education.

I will mention here that the majority of these studies and research papers talk about the 'potential' benefits of play and how play can support, contribute to, or help with the development of skills. They do not suggest that play will solve all of our attainment and development needs as teachers. McGuinness et al. (2014) even found that a play-based curriculum made no significant difference to the numeracy and literacy outcomes of young learners. It is for this reason that I advocate for a more mixed approach. Using play meets the developmental needs of your learners while also providing a teaching approach that will also meet their academic needs. It has been shown that a playful pedagogy can be more effective at developing holistic skills than a traditional, guided approach (Parker and Thomsen, 2019), and this indicates that a play-based pedagogy should be developed with care. Embracing a playful or play-based approach can increase engagement and motivation as well as develop many skills required for learning, life, and work, but some teacher-led input is required to ensure pupils are progressing and prepared for the next step on their learning journey.

Play can be used to engage learners and to provide inclusive learning for those learners who require some additional support. The principles of play allow learners to find their own way into their learning, perhaps with your support. Using the principles of play allows learners to put their own interests into their learning. Play should be accessible and available to all learners at the primary or elementary level of education, regardless of their age, ability, background, or any additional needs they may have.

Play can be a powerful tool to support learning. It can be used to incite curiosity, raise engagement, and ultimately raise attainment (Parker et al., 2022). It can also help children make sense of what we are trying to teach them and allow them to apply it to their own world. Why should this stop after the early years? Apart from anything else, play is fun. Playful learning engages children, and learning should be fun if we want children to pursue it independently and retain the information that we are teaching them.

When children play, on their own or together, they learn a whole raft of skills:

- Sharing
- Taking turns
- Solving problems
- Patience
- What they like/don't like
- Managing their emotions
- Winning/losing
- Risk-taking or avoidance
- Time management
- Using their imagination
- Conflict management
- How to work with others/entertain others
- Scientific Concepts (gravity, rotation, momentum . . .)
- How to be alone/entertain themselves
- Fairness (and that sometimes things aren't fair!)
- Understanding scientific concepts (gravity, rotation, momentum, etc.)
- Learning from mistakes
- Resilience

I could go on and on, but you get the idea.

The development of skills and the independent application of these skills are part of our job as teachers. They are perhaps not listed in the standards or outcomes we teach, but without them, our students cannot effectively learn and use what they have learned in other contexts. Some councils and authorities may even have a skills framework that you can refer to when monitoring the learning achieved by your pupils.

Play allows learners to put their learning into context. It could be a context of their choosing – a role-play activity or an imaginary game with a back story – or it could be a context you give them. Putting learning into a context and allowing learners the opportunity to apply their conceptual learning, preferably in a real-life context, gives them a reason for their learning. The depth of learning increases when you challenge learners to build and explore what angle of a ramp will allow Mr Smith to freewheel his car the maximum distance in order to save fuel compared with you asking learners to theorise how the angle of a ramp affects the speed of a car travelling down it.

The skills that can be developed through play are wide and varied. There is some debate over what constitutes play-based learning and whether this should include free play or play guided by teachers. As mentioned earlier, there is a difference between free play and play-based learning, and in an education system where attainment results are paramount, it is difficult to imagine a pedagogy completely free from teacher involvement. Even within this teacher involvement, there will be variation in the knowledge about play among teachers who may not have been formally trained in play practice or have undertaken different levels of training. Differences in the way it is planned for, facilitated, recorded, evaluated, built on. Nevertheless, the essence of play-based learning is that children learn while they are at play. This play looks different for every child. Learning can be achieved through a directed input where the teacher's goal is to use play to achieve a pre-determined, educational outcome (purpose-focused play), or it might be incidental learning acquired through self-determined activities and exploration (free play). Ideally, we should strive to have a mixture of both.

If you focus on what you want from the pupils, you can create some flexibility and playfulness in your approach. Do you really need everyone to complete the same activity to show you that they have understood it? I often use a working backwards model of planning used by Griffiths and Burns (2014). If we start by focussing on what we want our learners to achieve or understand, we then plan backwards from that point, creating learning opportunities and experiences that will guide them to that finish point. As long as our learners reach that point and have a full understanding of the concept that we want to teach them, how they get there can be variable, depending on the needs of the learners.

To illustrate what I mean by this, let me tell you about a lesson I did on rhyming.

Rhyming is something I knew that my class had covered before, so what I needed from them was evidence that they understood what rhyme was and could use it to create their own rhyming text. I could have delivered a lesson on poetry and asked them all to write me a rhyming poem. What I did instead was read *Oi Frog* by Kes Gray and Jim Field (2014) to the class. Following the reading of the book, I asked the class for other rhyming examples and where else we see rhyme (poems, other stories, songs). I then gave them 20 minutes to create something using rhyme to show me that they understood it. I got three songs, a rap, six poems, and a book. A pair of boys had written their own version of *Oi Frog*, involving every child in the class. This variation would not have happened if I had given a whole class instruction, telling them all exactly what rhyming activity I wanted them to do. It also allowed the class to differentiate themselves. They took on tasks that they felt able to do. And as a teacher, I much prefer the variety of marking different pieces of work rather than 30 identical pieces of differing quality.

And what if we took these principles of play – choice, motivation, and drive all coming from the learner themselves – and applied them to all aspects of learning? Are we not then looking at pupil voice, contextual understanding, transference, and application of skills? All are vital to raising attainment and engagement within our schools. If we reframe the idea of play, thinking of it as more of an approach that encourages learners to be more independent, curious, and self-driven, then it becomes more palatable in the upper stages. By changing some of the ways we approach our teaching, we create an ethos of play-based or playful learning – allowing pupils an element of choice in where or how they complete their work, opportunities for pupils to elaborate on something they have learned about and take an interest in, variation in the amount of teacher input provided to learners – these all encourage learners to drive their own learning in their own way. Create a space where exploration and investigation are encouraged, mistakes are a comfortable part of learning, and pupils feel safe to make suggestions and ask questions.

To do this, we need to focus on what we are asking of our learners, specifically, what we want them to learn. If I am teaching my class about punctuation and need them to demonstrate their understanding and application of punctuation in their writing, does it matter if it is written in pen or pencil? Handwritten or typed? Written as a story or a comic strip? As long as the key elements of punctuation that I am looking for are in evidence, the other elements can be chosen by the learners. Sometimes, we need to think a little bit outside the box to engage our learners. Instead of completing a planning sheet or mindmap template on setting the scene, perhaps they could create a scene with Lego, use Minecraft, or build a diorama. Instead of the class watching a video of life under the sea, try going underwater with Google Expeditions. Instead of times tables flashcards, create a rap or song about multiplication facts. Trying out different approaches encourages pupils to do the same, but it might help us find our playful side as well.

Another important element of play is that children make their activities relevant to them. Personal relevance is vital in helping learners understand new concepts and to transference and application of skills. When teaching bearings and directions, allow some exploration of the local area. Where is your house in relation to the school? Write some directions from your house to the local shop. Textbook examples are good for practise, but they don't provide a relevant link to real life. That's where we come in. I have invited pupils to write to me to persuade me to do something they would like for the Christmas term. The possibility of my acting on their writing made sure the requests were realistic, persuasive, and of the best quality they could be.

Giving your learners ownership of their learning and creating an environment where questions are encouraged and acted on makes pupils feel more included and responsible for their learning. Allow key questions from learners to lead to discussions and lessons. Allow children to drive the questioning and take charge of their own learning, and they will become more autonomous in their learning, research, and investigating. Hopefully, it will contribute to the whole development of the child as a successful learner.

Let's Keep Playing

In a previous life, I was a football (soccer) coach and was lucky enough to work with Manchester United Soccer Schools for several seasons. One of the things we were taught as coaches was to try and avoid coaching players during a game. Teach them everything you can during training, give them effective and inspiring team talks before matches, but avoid shouting instructions onto the pitch during the actual match.

It was only when I entered the world of teaching and began coaching the school team that I fully appreciated the importance of this coaching technique. I observed one coach repeatedly shout instructions to his players – "pass to the left", "close him down", "shoot!" At one point, I saw a young player receive a pass from his teammate and immediately look towards his coach to be told what to do. He was inevitably tackled and lost the ball. It was in that moment I realised the importance of not always telling learners what to do in allowing them to develop the application of their skills with at least some degree of independence. If we consistently tell our learners what to do, how to do it, and when to do it, they will lose their ability to make decisions for themselves and apply their learning independently when we are not there to support them.

> **Take Away**
>
> Opportunities to play, explore, and investigate independently can support children in developing a raft of skills, including problem-solving, negotiating, communicating, time-management, and resilience. Play can support physical, emotional, and social development as well as language skills, cognitive abilities, and critical thinking. It can foster independence, and when tailored to meet the age and stage of the learners involved, these opportunities can help prepare children for their next stage of development.

References

Broadhead, P., Howard, J., and Wood, E. (Eds). (2010). *Play and Learning in the Early Years: From Research to Practice*. London: SAGE Publishing.

Christie, J.F., and Roskos, K.A. (2006). Standards, Science and the Role of Play in Early Literacy Education. In Singer, D.G., Golinkoff, R.M., and Hirsh-Pasek, K. (Eds) *Play=Learning: How Play Motivates and Enhances Children's Cognitive and Social-Emotional Growth*. New York, NY: Oxford University Press.

Danniels, E., and Pyle, A. (2018). *Defining Play-Based Learning*. OISE University of Toronto, Canada. http://ceril.net/index.php/articulos?id=594

Dewar, G. (2023). *The Cognitive Benefits of Play: Effects on the Learning Brain*. www.parentingscience.com/benefits-of-play.html

Fleer, M. (2021). *Play in the Early Years* (3rd Edition). Cambridge, UK: Cambridge University Press.

Ginsburg, K.R., American Academy of Pediatrics Committee on Communications, and American Academy of Pediatrics Committee on Psychosocial Aspects of Child and Family Health. (2007). The Importance of Play in Promoting Healthy Child Development and Maintaining Strong Parent-Child Bonds. *Pediatrics* 119(1): 182-191.

Goldstein, J. (2012). *Play in Children's Development, Health and Well-Being*. Brussels: Toy Industries of Europe.

Gray, K., and Field, J. (2014). *Oi Frog!* London: Hodder Children's Books.

Griffiths, A., and Burns, M. (2014). *Teaching Backwards*. United Kingdom Carmarthen, Wales: Crown House Publishing.

Koepp, A.E., Gershoff, E.T., Castelli, D.M., and Bryan, A.E. (2022). Preschoolers' Executive Functions Following Indoor and Outdoor Free Play. *Trends in Neuroscience and Education* 28: 100182.

Krechevsky, M., Baldwin, M., Rodriguez, M.C., Christensen, L., Jorgensen, M., Jorgensen, O., Krishnadas, S., Overgaard, S., and Rabenhoj, T. (2019). Frankly It's a Gamble: What Happens When Middle School Students Compose Their Own Schedules? *Scottish Educational Review* 51(2): 50-64.

Lubans, D.R., Morgan, P.J., Cliff, D.P., Barnett, L.M., and Okely, A.D. (2010). Fundamental Movement Skills in Children and Adolescents: Review of the Associated Health Benefits. *Sports Medicine* 40(12): 1019-1035.

McGuinness, C., Sproule, L., Bojke, C., Trew, K., and Walsh, G. (2014, October). Impact of a Play-Based Curriculum in the First Two Years of Primary School: Literacy and Numeracy Outcomes Over Seven Years. *British Educational Research Journal* 40(5): 772-795.

Nestor, O., and Moser, C.S. (2018). The Importance of Play. *Journal of Occupational Therapy, Schools, and Early Intervention* 11(3): 247-262.

Palmer, S. (2019). Why Scotland Needs a Kindergarten Stage (3-7 Years). *Scottish Educational Review* 51(2): 87-95.

Parker, R., and Thomsen, B.S. (2019). *Learning Through Play at School: A Study of Playful Integrated Pedagogies that Foster Children's Holistic Skills Development in the Primary School Classroom*. Billund: LEGO Foundation.

Parker, R., Thomsen, B.S., and Berry, A. (2022). Learning Through Play at School - A Framework for Policy and Practice. *Secondary Teacher Education* 7. https://doi.org/10.3389/feduc.2022.751801

Riley, J.G., and Jones, R.B. (2010). Acknowledging Learning Through Play in the Primary Grades. *Childhood Education* 86(3): 146-149.

Schlesinger, M.A., Hassinger-Das, B., Zosh, J.M., Sawyer, J., Evans, N., and Hirsh-Pasek, K. (2020). Cognitive Behavioral Science Behind the Value of Play: Leveraging Everyday Experiences to Promote Play, Learning, and Positive Interactions. *Journal of Infant, Child, and Adolescent Psychotherapy* 19(2): 202-216.

Sheridan, M.D. (2011). *Play in Early Childhood: From Birth to Six Years* (3rd Edition), Revised and Updated by Howard, J. and Alderson, D. London: Routledge.

Walsh, G.M., McGuinness, C., Sproule, L., and Trew, K. (2010). Implementing a Play-Based and Developmentally Appropriate Curriculum in Northern Ireland Primary Schools: What Lessons Have We Learned? *An International Research Journal* 30(1): 53-66.

Wood, E.A. (2013). Free Choice and Free Play in Early Childhood Education: Troubling the Discourse. *International Journal of Early Years Education* 22(1): 4-18.

Yogman, M., Garner, A., Hutchison, M.D., and Hirsh-Pasek, K. (2018). The Power of Play: A Pediatric Role in Enhancing Development in Young Children. *American Academy of Pediatrics* 142(3): e20.

Young, E. (2021, August 13). *Let the Children Play: Research on the Importance of Play, Digested.* The British Psychological Society. https://digest.bps.org.uk/2021/08/13/let-the-children-play-research-on-the-importance-of-play-digested/

Zachariou, A., and Whitebread, D. (2015). Musical Play and Self-Regulation: Does Musical Play Allow for the Emergence of Self-Regulatory Behaviours? *International Journal of Play* 5(1): 116-135.

3 Play in the Early Years and Beyond

Early Years vs Upper Stages

As mentioned, and referenced in Chapter 2, play in the early years is recognised to provide children with important benefits for their progression and development. As learners move through school, they develop different skills. As they get older, there is a need for more transferable skills and a certain level of independence.

Learning through play for older learners needs an approach that builds on the practice of the early years and doesn't simply replicate it. There needs to be appropriate challenges and opportunities for students to develop initiative and autonomy over their own learning. While there may still be features of the play you will see in the early years, the activities need to be more tailored to the age and stage of the pupils involved. Older children can take more control of the direction of their learning as they have a clearer idea of their interests and challenges.

The play-based curriculum was designed to bring about positive effects, not only on the immediate learning experiences of the children in the first years of primary school but also to create a positive learning foundation to sustain learning and progress in school over the longer term (McGuinness et al., 2014). The research on the effects of learning through play tends to concentrate on play in children up to around 8 years of age. This could be linked to Piaget's theory that the concrete operational stage begins at around 7 years of age when children begin to problem solve, reason, and apply logic (Lefa, 2014). Free play opportunities are often made available to learners until they reach this stage of their development. I would argue, though, that the emergence of reasoning, logic, and problem-solving skills is the ideal time to offer some play principles. It gives learners opportunities to explore these skills further and apply them contextually and in a real-life way that is meaningful to them.

Finding research on the effects of play-related learning on older pupils is hard to find, but there is some out there, either specifically on the benefits of play for older learners or highlighting the fact that the positive effects of play can be felt by learners of all ages (Dearybury and Jones, 2020; McKendrick, 2019a, 2019b; Parker et al., 2022). The field is growing, though, and providing older learners with play-based opportunities is proving to be just as beneficial if done in the right way. There is little evidence to explain why this area is less well explored, but the pressure on teachers to raise attainment and produce results to show progress in learning would probably explain the drop in play opportunities as pupils progress through

20 A Play-Based Pedagogy

Figure 3.1 Place Value Dice

the education system. However, a quick search on any social media platform for 'Play in the Upper Stages' will produce a realm of teachers bringing play into their upper stages classes. But is it enough to simply transfer play experiences that work in the early years into the upper stages or is a different approach more effective? Play is still a valuable learning tool beyond the early years. There are elements of play that encourage learning and life skills that will be crucial as our learners progress through their education to a more independent and self-motivating environment.

Challenge

Play can be a tricky topic to facilitate challenge with. Essentially it is something that children do independently, and as we have seen, true play involves very little, if any, adult interference. Some educators believe that children can lead their own learning through play and are reluctant to interfere with this as it diminishes the value of their play. This can lead to a somewhat laid-back approach to play opportunities, but while simply providing play-based activities might facilitate the development of emotional and social aspects of learning, it will not necessarily promote cognitive and metacognitive processes (Walsh et al., 2010). Developing the academic aspects of learning and ensuring progression is more complex. Many educators believe play and academic achievement are at opposite ends of the learning spectrum but if facilitated and supported correctly, play can bring about deeper learning and understanding, but it does require some adult involvement. The trick is to find a balance between providing the opportunity for play, with its exploration, investigation, engagement, and discovery, along with academic challenge and progress.

It is important to ensure that the play opportunities provided create challenges for learners. I talk to my class about their comfort zone, where they are relaxed, and their stretch zone, where they can learn. I try to provide play opportunities that allow my learners to put their learning into a real context. Throughout my years of teaching, a common frustration amongst teachers is that pupils find it difficult to transfer the skills that they learn into different situations and, as a result, embed their learning securely. How many of us have taken on a class who claim to have never learned about dividing before? Or to have never seen speech marks before. We know they have; they just haven't retained it effectively or can recall it confidently.

Providing a context for learners to explore and play with the concepts we teach will help them make sense of them in real life and hopefully retain and recall them when required. Create an environment that invites questions, investigation, and curiosity and allows your learners to access activities that support your teaching but also meet their interests and needs. I have a 'Question Wall' for my class to stick Post-Its with questions or ideas. I try to either answer them or allow time and resources for the pupils to research them independently. If you have this ethos in your classroom, learners will independently seek to find out, explore, and investigate, enhancing their learning styles while using the play principles of free choice, intrinsic motivation, and personal drive. Children will learn from their own investigations, but they will also learn from their peers and their environment if they are given the opportunity to. Support your learners in reflecting on their learning and progress to revisit it and build on it. I have seen a noticeable increase in pupils asking me if I have marked their work yet – they are keen to see how they have done and see if they have improved. Empower them to lead aspects of their own learning, and they will engage and be motivated.

It is important to remember that the process is much more important than the product. Teaching children how to research a historical person that interests them, take notes, and turn their notes into something else, whether that's a poster, report, or presentation, is much more meaningful than the production of 30 reports on William Wallace. Yes, they have all demonstrated that they can research facts about a historical figure, but the first approach means the pupils will learn from each other, remember it better, and it is much more interesting for you to assess as well!

Applying Their Learning into Contexts

One of the main aspects of play is the opportunity to apply learning into a context. Beyond the early years, this becomes important in the deepening of learning and understanding as more complex concepts are introduced. Teaching learners about the concept of percentages can be done with a textbook and some word problems. But can they apply their learning in their own lives? Their understanding is deepened when they know why they need to learn about them and can try out their learning in a safe, realistic context. We want children to see their learning as meaningful and useful, so we need to give it meaning. Once we have taught the concept of percentages, why not provide a shopping role-play opportunity with discount cards that give 20% off? Or an activity involving online shopping where you offer to pay for 50%, and your learners must cover the rest. Create opportunities to use learning.

Beyond the early years, a play-based approach is quite often utilised by teachers supporting learners with additional needs or barriers to their learning. The reason for this is that play is accessible, it is inclusive, and it is engaging. Isn't this what we want to offer all our learners? Learning that is accessible, inclusive, and engaging?

I have taught both in the mainstream classroom and as a support for learning (ASN) teacher. Learners in a mainstream class, watching their peers be taken out for something that is inevitably considered more interesting or more exciting, leads to resentment. There is an element of mystery or unfairness if someone in your class 'gets to do Messy Maths' while the rest of the class does some textbook work. But what if everyone got the opportunity to try Messy Maths at least once? I tried it with my Primary 5 class (Year 6). The next time a child was taken out for some Messy Maths during our Numeracy slot, we all did Messy Maths. The mystery was gone. "Is that all it is?!" was the response from one group. "This is amazing!" from another (the group who usually required the most support from me). "Meh!" from a third. And from then on, when we did Numeracy, a messy option was occasionally offered but, interestingly, rarely taken. Now, the child who was taken out for support was no longer looked upon with resentment or jealousy, and the class felt more involved, knowing what the support looked like.

What I learned from this is that when play is dangled near children as an unattainable thing, they want it badly. When it is present continuously, they only access it when they need it.

Following the effects of the coronavirus pandemic on our young people's education, professionals have been looking at alternative approaches to support our children and young people to offset any detrimental effects on attainment (Scottish Government, 2021). Reports show that play could be vital in supporting children in understanding and recovering from the effects of traumatic events (Riley and Jones, 2010; Young, 2021), and this may have played a part in the change in pedagogical approach that is happening. Play offers the opportunity for young people to process events, to link ideas and thoughts, to find support in others who can relate. It also provides an opportunity to process other learning and experiences, too.

Play as a tool for supporting learning is widely recognised as an effective learning pedagogy and is used in the early years. However, policies on play generally do not mention an age restriction on play. They usually state that **all** children or young people need opportunities for play and that playful learning is necessary in all schools, nursery, primary, secondary, and special, which brings us very neatly back to the subject of how play might change beyond the early years.

I see many posts on social media purportedly displaying play in the upper years, but when looking for ideas online, please be mindful of the level of play you are striving for. Many of the posts I have come across show a set task, with set instructions, with an outcome envisaged by the teacher. Or a Tuff Tray with resources set out and a specific task set for the class. These contain valuable learning for the class and would be considered playful learning. To be considered play, at least some elements of the activity would need to be optional – not always appropriate in an upper stages class where attainment and task completion are crucial! If we are considering the definition of play mentioned previously, it should be unstructured and child-led, not explicitly planned by the teacher, with a single, adult-guided outcome. But we can achieve a balance. Consider an art lesson where the learning intention is related to the recognition of detail. You could model a lesson on drawing a bowl of fruit you have displayed, emphasising the shapes, proportions, shadows, and then provide the class with their paper to produce 25 pictures of a bowl of fruit from different angles. Or, you could start your lesson by discussing the importance of detail, emphasising shape, proportion, shadow. Then, show the class a range of artwork displaying such detail but from a range of styles using a range of materials (Michaelangelo, Dali, van Gogh, and the ancient Egyptian hieroglyphs all contain a lot of detail in their artwork). Now recap the importance of the detail elements and allow your learners to create their own artwork. You will be rewarded with around 25 very different pieces of art, and you will have allowed your learners an element of play in their learning – personal choice and, hopefully, some intrinsic motivation.

Sometimes, the concept of play doesn't sit very well with those considering learners beyond the early years. The idea of free choice and fun are somewhat removed from the image of attainment scores and progression. However, if we kept the principles, opportunities, and pupil-led aspects but gave play a different name, would we, as upper-stage educators, feel better about employing it as a pedagogy? Developmentally Appropriate Teaching? Real-Life Application of Learning? Independent Learning Experiences? Contextualised Opportunities? Active Learning? Personally, I think of it as all of the above! In providing materials and resources to which the pupils have free access, they are putting what they have learned into a context that helps them understand it, retain it and hopefully be able to apply it in real life. Whatever you want to call it, and however it looks in your classroom, the principles remain the same. Ability levels, interests, strengths, areas for development, barriers to learning – these all differ more widely as children progress through the school as learners develop their own styles of learning and interests. As such, play can look very different from one child to the next, even in the same class.

On completion of a task, I have offered learners opportunities to apply their learning in a range of ways. Given the option, I have observed situations in which several learners regularly chose to play with the games or with junk modelling while others chose to write a story or request to complete additional calculations from their textbook and then mark each other's work with coloured pens. All these activities constitute play as they were freely chosen, intrinsically motivated and personally directed, and appropriate to the needs of the learner. As their teacher, it was eye opening for me to see that some learners chose to apply their learning to further textbook work. They were selecting activities that met their learning needs at that time. As learners become aware of their strengths and abilities as well as their learning needs, they also embrace challenge and success. Following a data interpretation lesson, I have seen pupils ask to survey their own classmates and create graphs; after a grammar lesson, some will write their own short story while others listen to an audiobook. It allows them the freedom to choose and explore their learning in their own way.

Make-believe is often thought of as a younger child's activity, and pretending and role play are rife in the early years – dressing up, doll's houses, dinosaurs, puppets, there are plenty of opportunities for fantasy and pretending.

Much less so in a classroom further up the school. There's no need for it, surely. It's a time to be more realistic and practical, not pretending and dressing up.

When I teach word problems in Numeracy, I talk to the learners about visualisation. It is often the case that students can more easily grasp the concept of simple calculations but have more difficulty solving a worded problem, particularly if there is more than one step to the solution.

24 *A Play-Based Pedagogy*

To illustrate, I am fairly confident that almost all of my class could solve these calculations when as laid out:

1) What is ¼ of 60?
2) Now subtract this answer from 60. What do you have left?
3) What is 20% of your answer to Q2?
4) Take your answer to Q3 away from your answer to Q2 – what do you have left?

But a few would struggle if faced with the problem:

> Barbara goes shopping with £60, spends ¼ of this in the first shop she visits, and then spends 20% of her remaining money in the second shop. How much money will she have going home?

I believe this is more difficult for many of our learners as they lose the ability to pretend and make-believe as they move through the school. They don't know Barbara; her shopping practices don't mean anything to them, so trying to work out what she does with her money is tricky.

Imagine, though, if we provided more opportunities for pretending and role-playing throughout their learning. Facing a 4-step problem like this would be less daunting as they perhaps pull out £60 from the play money pile, use blocks to represent shops, and do some messy calculations with chalk pens on their desks. Or even ask a peer to be a shopkeeper as they act out the scenario, solving the problem together.

A simple adjustment is changing the names in your word problems to those of the class (or their friends or family), and it can make a huge difference as the question becomes more relevant to them and easier to visualise immediately.

Figure 3.2 Shop Role Play

For play to be appropriate for older learners, the pupils need to be involved in the planning, and the adults need to respond to their ideas and interests. Contexts need to be relevant and meaningful to the learners. Resources need to be open and flexible for learners to use in their own ways. When you plan your topics or themes for the term, do you plan for your class, or do you allow them some input into what they would like to find out about or how they would like to learn or show their learning?

We do need to bear in mind, though, that our upper-stages classes are preparing for high school, where there is likely to be little opportunity for play as we generally know it. There will be opportunities for self-driven study, self-motivation, problem-solving, working collaboratively, and independent learning. We can use our contextual learning opportunities to develop these skills, and furthermore, the play principles can be used to develop skills such as independence, patience, and teamwork, and encourage learners to investigate, speculate, compare, explore, problem-solve, and many more. We can cultivate these skills in our young learners through play but in a way that allows them to use them in a different context as they progress through their education. It can help with their depth of understanding and recall of information, as well as their retrieval and retention. It also provides us with opportunities for high-quality assessment – assessing understanding in a new context is not the same as understanding shown on a paper test.

Take Away

Before providing opportunities for play for any learners, it is important to consider their educational and developmental needs. Play activities designed for the early years will not necessarily challenge or engage older learners for very long. Equally, play activities designed for 12-year-olds may not meet the needs of every learner in your P7/Year 6 class. It is important to provide play opportunities that include challenges and opportunities for developmentally appropriate independent learning to allow for progress and ongoing learning.

References

Dearybury, J., and Jones, J. (2020). *The Playful Classroom: The Power of Play for All Ages*. New Jersey: Jossey-Bass.

Lefa, B. (2014). The Piaget Theory of Cognitive Development: An Education Implication. *Educational Psychology* 1(1): 9.

McGuinness, C., Sproule, L., Bojke, C., Trew, K., and Walsh, G. (2014, October). Impact of a Play-Based Curriculum in the First Two Years of Primary School: Literacy and Numeracy Outcomes Over Seven Years. *British Educational Research Journal* 40(5): 772-795.

McKendrick, J. (2019a). Shall the Twain Meet? Prospects for a Playfully Play-Full Scottish Education. *Scottish Educational Review* 51(2): 3-13.

McKendrick, J. (2019b). Realising the Potential of Play in Scottish Education. *Scottish Educational Review* 51(2): 137-142.

Parker, R., Thomsen, B.S., and Berry, A. (2022). Learning Through Play at School – A Framework for Policy and Practice. *Secondary Teacher Education* 7. https://doi.org/10.3389/feduc.2022.751801

Riley, J.G., and Jones, R.B. (2010). Acknowledging Learning Through Play in the Primary Grades. *Childhood Education* 86(3): 146-149.

Scottish Government. (2021). *Progress Review of Scotland's Play Strategy 2021: Play in a Covid-19 Context*. www.playscotland.org/wp-content/uploads/Play-Scotland-Play-Strategy-Review-Play-in-Covid-2021.pdf

Walsh, G.M., McGuinness, C., Sproule, L., and Trew, K. (2010). Implementing a Play-Based and Developmentally Appropriate Curriculum in Northern Ireland Primary Schools: What Lessons Have We Learned? *An International Research Journal* 30(1): 53-66.

Young, E. (2021, August 13). *Let the Children Play: Research on the Importance of Play, Digested*. The British Psychological Society. https://digest.bps.org.uk/2021/08/13/let-the-children-play-research-on-the-importance-of-play-digested/

4 Putting the Principles into Action

How Can We Play?

Play opportunities can be offered to your learners in a variety of ways. The phrase 'Continuous Provision' generally refers to having resources and areas set out in the classroom all the time to encourage learning through play and exploration. These resources should be accessible to the children in the classroom and should stay more or less the same throughout the school year. They might include things like blocks, art materials, and puzzles. There may also be topical or contextual areas that change from time to time to support learning about a particular theme – Fairy Tales or People Who Help Us, for example.

Beyond the early years, free play becomes very difficult to find time for. Play can be a constant presence in your classroom through play trays, a Tuff Tray, or games and activities that are always left out. Depending on your class, there may be certain times of the day or designated times of the week that are more suitable for play activities. You may have a play-based classroom or a separate room where children go to play.

How you allow learners to access play is also important. I would urge you not to provide play as a fun activity for those who have completed their work, as this often results in learners rushing through their 'learning' to get to the play, and the work produced is rarely of the best quality. Play and learning should not be seen as separate things. I believe a constant presence allows learners to relax into their play-based learning and not rush to get to the activities in fear they will be taken away or insecure feelings of when they will play again. You can provide play-based activities throughout the week as part of a specific learning objective or with a more general target of allowing the children to explore, investigate, or simply enjoy some time together. I will provide some examples of these activities later in the book.

If we remember, the main principles of play are that it is freely chosen, intrinsically motivated, and personally driven, as well as fun. In an infant classroom, these principles come into play naturally as carefully selected activities and materials are left out to encourage younger learners to engage with them willingly and voluntarily. In a classroom further up the school, the play principles are less easy to find as there is a curriculum to follow, assessments to prepare for, attainment results to achieve, and learners to prepare for their next step in education.

So, let's consider all these learning targets and attainment targets and look at how these principles might look throughout the school.

DOI: 10.4324/9781003486602-6

Freely Chosen

Allowing your learners some choice in their learning might be a bit daunting for you. As teachers, we like having a lot of control over what our students do and learn. We feel like we can keep everything going in the right direction if we have an influence over what is happening.

The best way to help our learners raise their attainment and improve their understanding is to keep them engaged. And the best way to keep them engaged is to find something that interests them and empower them to have some ownership over their learning. Choice enables them to do this. This does not mean a choice of everything they are going to do. It means:

> Choice over how they can demonstrate their understanding of a given subject.
> Choice over what order they will complete a set of given activities.
> Choice over where they will sit (or stand) to complete their work.
> Choice over who they will work with.
> Choice over which questions they answer.

I am not for one second suggesting you offer this level of choice in your classroom all the time. Too much choice can lead to chaos! However, if you focus on the outcome that you are looking for, you can consider where you can offer some choice without negatively affecting your results. If I need a class to show me their understanding of multiplication by two-digit numbers, does it really matter whether they complete questions 1–5 in their textbook in the order given? Do I really need them to write all their answers in their jotter, or is it okay for them to write their answers on the table with a chalk pen? Do I mind if they stand up to complete this work? Do I mind who they work with? Do I mind if they verbally explain their answers rather than write them down?

If the answer to some of these questions is no, then I can allow my learners an element of choice in their learning activity.

For example, writing can be a struggle for some learners and a barrier to the completion of a task. If you have a learner (or learners) who might be reluctant to engage in activities involving writing, perhaps you could consider:

- Building a representation with blocks
- Talk to your shoulder partner
- A game
- Video reflections or interviews
- Scavenger hunt to find facts
- Putting information cards in the correct order
- Creating a song or rap
- Online explorations (Maps or Google Earth)
- Message or email responses
- Dramatic readings or recounts of events
- Virtual visits to museums or attractions (many zoos have online tours)
- Draw your answers
- Voice recordings or podcasts

The point is that learners can show their learning in a range of ways. Occasionally, we can be guilty of looking at their reading or writing ability as a measure of how much they have learned when there are so many other ways to look at it.

A word of caution, though, this is not an invitation to give your learners choice over everything they do in your class. As we prepare them for the next stage of their education, one of the many skills learners need to develop is the ability to follow instructions and listen to the adults instructing them. While I have mentioned giving pupils a choice over where they sit, I still have boundaries within this. For example, there are certain learners who would not do well sitting next to each other or other learners who need to sit near the front of the class to see the board properly. In any circumstance like this, I always explain to the pupils involved why I am imposing this boundary, and I involve them in the decision. "I think we know that sitting next to Child A isn't the best idea for you and won't help you complete the work to the best of your ability, but I am happy for you to sit here or over there instead". "Remember, we discussed how important it is for you to sit facing the board, so we're going to keep your seat where it is, but why don't you invite Child X to sit next to you?" Or we sit in our Home Seats for Numeracy, but you might get the chance to work together for art this afternoon or be in the same team for PE later. These responses are always better than a flat "no".

There are many ways you can offer children choices that give them the sense of empowerment and control that is so important for engagement, but maintain your control over the safety of the class and the quality of their work. Instead of saying, "You can choose where you sit for this task", try, "You can sit or stand at your desk to complete this task", or, "You need to stay at your group, but you can choose where at the table you sit".

Hopefully, your learners will develop an understanding of why some decisions are up to them and why you still need to guide them in other decisions. They are still children, after all. Perhaps, over time, you will be able to give them control over more decisions as you become more confident that they will make positive choices for their learning.

It is important for learners to develop their decision-making skills. If we make every decision for them – this is where you sit, this is who you work with, this is the work I want you to complete, and here is how I want you to complete it – are we properly equipping them for the real world? I remember being asked to pick a book for a book report and choose a topic for a class talk in my First Year of high school English. Choices. In History, we were given a homework task to research a particular discovery (The Body in the Bog, if memory serves me correctly). We had to make our own decisions about how we were going to research it and where we would find the information. Choices. In Modern Studies, we had to work in groups to present our own business ideas to the class for a school fundraiser. Choices. In the outside world, peers may offer them substances or invitations to activities that carry an element of risk to their health or wellbeing. Choices.

Encouraging young learners to think for themselves while supporting them in making the right choices and creating a safe environment to make some wrong ones allows them to develop the confidence to hopefully make good choices in their future years.

Intrinsically Motivated

Intrinsic motivation is doing an activity simply for the satisfaction of doing it, not for an external reward or consequence. Teachers can support their learners to become more intrinsically motivated by providing options, setting goals, and embracing their interests and curiosities. If learners don't care about the subject they are learning or how they perform in it, they are not motivated to complete the tasks with much degree of effort. Many teachers, myself included, will have attempted to motivate learners with stickers, points, reward schemes, or any other system designed to inspire our class with material rewards from the outside. This only works short-term and does not prepare our learners for future education where no one is handing out stickers for attending lectures or turning up to work on time! We need to help our students find ways to motivate themselves.

We can do this by providing our students with a supportive, quality learning environment that empowers them and encourages them to be independent and make good choices about their learning. Support them to be proud of their work – display it, send notes home, take photos of it – help them to see that the end result is, sometimes, reward enough. Share their successes with home, allow them to take pictures of work they are proud of, send copies home with them, and invite parents and families in to share in your work. If a learner seems a bit apathetic about the reaction from home, send them to the management team with a piece of work they should be proud of or another member of staff that the pupil cares about. Many of my students have been proud to show off their successes to a member of the support staff whose opinions they care about (often someone who worked with them when they were much younger!) and who will make an appropriate fuss over their achievements.

While this might seem somewhat like an extrinsic reward, something we are trying to avoid, children are still developing their inner voice. Hearing someone else tell them they are impressed or proud of their work will eventually become secondary to the pride they feel within themselves on hearing these words.

If we can link learning to contexts that allow learners to make connections to it and engage with it, the learning will have more meaning for the students. It also helps them to apply what they have learned in their own lives.

As well as this, expressing our own enthusiasm for learning will also transfer to our learners and support them in finding their own passion in their learning, too. If we appear interested and curious, it sparks a curiosity in our learners. Teachers who exhibit their own passion for learning will transfer this to their students and open up a world of possibilities (Valerio, 2012). I will often ponder aloud about things, discuss possibilities with the class, and inevitably look it up together as we explore a concept as a class. I want them to be interested in learning new things, so I need to model that for them.

Personally Driven

I am driven by setting myself targets and making lists. I have lists everywhere. I enjoy the sense of achievement as I score items from my to-do lists or tick things off my shopping list. I have even been guilty of adding things to a list that I have already done just so I can score it off! This drives me to keep working on my tasks.

Find out what drives your learners. If they are interested in test scores, then share that with them. Give them scores when you mark their work. I have taught learners who became very excited by percentage scores and grades (which we didn't do as standard in our school). I would grade their work accordingly with a comment as to how they could achieve an even higher grade. A piece of writing might have a score of 72% or a 'B' with the comment, "Don't forget to include some adverbs and adjectives to create more descriptive writing". The individual grades might not contribute much to the overall attainment record of this learner, but the mark and comment drives them to improve their writing next time.

We have also used graphs of assessment scores that I share with the learners to show them a visual of their progress. I regularly discuss with them how they are getting on, how they feel about their progress, what they would like to challenge themselves with next, and how we are going to achieve that goal.

Find out from your learners where they would like their learning to go. There will undoubtedly be some limitations to where you can allow them to take it, but if the class has been learning about life cycles and some students would like to plant their own seeds to see what would happen, can you facilitate this for them? Allowing a little bit of flexibility in your planning to let your learners have a say in what they would like to learn or how they would like to learn will go a big way in driving their learning forwards.

These principles all link together quite well. By asking your learners what they are interested in and listening to them when they tell you, you are empowering them to drive their learning, have some choice in what or how they learn, and develop some pride in their completed work. And striving to feel more of this internal pride in their achievements and accomplishments is what will drive and motivate our students to choose to try, engage, and keep learning.

Take Away

Using the play principles does not mean simply allowing children to play freely all the time. The principles of choice, self-drive, and intrinsic motivation can be applied in any area of the curriculum in any number of lessons you deem appropriate. Be selective about how you apply this, knowing your class, your resources, and your setting. Always keep in mind that the opportunities you provide should be designed to meet your learners' needs as far as possible, but integrating the play principles will engage, drive, and motivate your learners.

References

Valerio, K. (2012). Intrinsic Motivation in the Classroom. *Journal of Student Engagement: Education Matters* 2(1): 30-35.

5 Barriers and Solutions

Occasionally, we might come across a resistance towards play pedagogy. Play-based learning is not universally accepted by all educators as the best tool that can meet all learners' needs, especially beyond the early years. Perhaps understandably. I say "understandably" because we base our opinions on our own experiences and what we see and hear from others. Until I tried it out myself, I struggled to see how the benefits of a pedagogy associated with children in the early years could transfer to older learners. I saw the word 'play' so often linked with younger learners that it was hard to conceive this approach in a Primary 7 or Year 6 classroom, especially where learners are preparing for the transition to high school and beyond. My advice to anyone considering something new, though, is to try it out yourself before you form a firm opinion.

We all know teachers are busy people. We have a lot on our plates. If you're looking at changing things or trying something new, there is no shortage of reasons not to bother. Any teacher who has never tried it (and even some who have!) will tell you several reasons that it won't/can't/shouldn't work. So, I have come up with some reasons why a play-based approach might be perceived as an unrealistic idea. But I'm also going to ask you to look at this another way. What if contextual opportunities became part of your teaching and could raise engagement in your classroom, thereby making your teaching practice easier and/or more enjoyable? What if it could also raise attainment and independence? If you are already sold on the idea of play for all stages, you might already have some solutions ready to tackle these barriers, and it can help convince colleagues if you go with a solution-focussed approach. If you are not convinced yet (firstly, thank you for reading this book!), here are some things that it might be helpful to consider:

Problem: Attainment

We are under ongoing and increasing pressure to raise attainment and bridge any gaps in learning. Teachers across the world have attainment-related targets set for their learners and a degree of pressure to meet the needs of all learners, support where it is required, and challenge where it is appropriate. The focus needs to be on ensuring learners are being challenged and progressing through the benchmarks and standards. The requirement to provide data to show these results means any change in pedagogy needs to have positive results that are robustly evidenced.

Inspectors visiting any school will be looking for data. And attainment levels that prove that we are doing our jobs well.

Solution

If used effectively, the play principles can be utilised to create contextual learning opportunities that contribute towards raising attainment, not taking learners away from their formal learning. If current reports about the potential benefits of play for ALL children are held to be true, it can add support to their learning, which can help deepen understanding and raise attainment, engagement, and learner wellbeing. If used correctly (read: not just letting the pupils do whatever they want, whenever they want!), opportunities for play and application of learning in context can support the development of independence, problem-solving, communication, enquiry, teamwork. . . . Transferring these skills into more traditional learning activities will have a tremendous impact on our attainment levels. The increased engagement and independence are just a bonus!

Problem: Introducing Something New

The introduction of new or innovative programmes is often met with resistance. Not another initiative that I have to get my head around?! Once you have been teaching for a few years, you become accustomed to new things coming and going with a certain regularity. If you have been teaching for more than five years, I can almost guarantee that you have seen a new initiative be brought in with some fanfare, training, and paperwork, only to disappear a few years later! Some new initiatives stick. Others come and go, and we move on to the next one. It is understandable that when something new comes along, there will be some that regard it with a certain degree of scepticism. Not to mention that the implementation of anything new usually comes with some kind of introductory period requiring meetings, discussions, changing resources, and who knows what else?

Solution

Henry Ford famously said, "If you always do what you've always done, you'll always get what you always got". If we never try something new, then you can't expect anything to change. Change is inevitable, especially if we are looking for things to improve. We'll never know how good something could be if we don't try it. It is our responsibility as class teachers to provide an education that meets the needs of the learners in our classroom. Research shows us that play helps the brain grow and develop in ways that will benefit every area of the curriculum. It also allows an opportunity to meet the needs of several learning styles in one go, providing its own differentiation through the pupil-directed approach. You could be the one bringing new and innovative changes to the way things are taught in your school. Be the change you want to see!

Problem: Time

When in the world are we supposed to fit play into our already crammed timetables? The curriculum, as it is, already fills our week, and with visitors, assemblies, trips, and all manner of extra things, there just isn't time to start bringing in something else.

Beyond the age of about 7, there is little time to allow pupils to simply play. The week becomes filled with literacy, numeracy, and progressive lessons that will allow these learners to reach their benchmarks in a timely manner. There are deadlines and benchmarks to meet.

And when am I going to have time to find resources, set up play opportunities, and tidy up after them? There are just not enough hours in the day.

Solution

The initial set-up might take some time, but setting up your classroom always does. If you start the academic year with a play or contextual pedagogy in mind, this will help your time management in the long run. And older pupils will be more than able to help set up their own contextualised areas with you in the first week of term. Once everything is in place, make it part of your routine for pupils to tidy things away or give certain pupils responsibilities for organising the resources and cleaning up after use. I have found investing in some nice-smelling washing-up liquid and some cheap spray bottles has worked wonders! Cleaning up after yourself is a life skill we should all be expecting from our students.

And play doesn't have to be an add-on to your timetable. It can be part of it. In your Friday morning Numeracy slot, make it a more playful session with a times table quiz or some short number games that the class rotates around. There are certain times of the day or week that lend themselves to opportunities to play, investigate, or explore in a more independent way – as a class after completing a non-negotiable task, just before lunch, the end of the day, Friday afternoons. It can be free play or more structured, curricular-linked play, depending on what is appropriate, but both are valid forms. You can timetable it or allow opportunities when appropriate. Whatever suits you and the needs of your class is the right approach.

Problem: Packed Curriculum

As already mentioned, the teaching curriculum is pretty packed. If we teach Literacy and Numeracy or Maths daily, meet our targeted hours of quality PE, and include sufficient Health and Wellbeing to make sure that all our learners' emotional needs are being met, then you add in Expressive Arts, Religious Education, Technologies, Sciences, and Social Studies as well as introducing an additional Language – is that not enough?! Not to mention making sure we meet all the standards or benchmarks required and teaching it to a good standard so that students are engaged and making good progress in all areas.

Solution

Learning through play or a context should be part of your curriculum, not an add-on. I am not suggesting we try to shoehorn this into an already busy curriculum, but, instead, to offer opportunities for children of all ages to access play to support their learning. We already plan for Numeracy, why not make one of your lessons a contextualised numeracy or problem-solving challenge? Or have Numeracy games and activities available for those who need them for further application or need a short brain break?

Consider a simple game that involves a group of learners, let's say Monopoly. When played properly during this game, the following experiences and outcomes or standards are being addressed:

Maths and Numeracy (money, budgeting, giving change), Chance and Certainty (dice rolling), Social Relationships (turn-taking, communication, negotiating), Managing Emotions (frustration, excitement, disappointment, etc.), Listening, and Talking (communicating with peers).

Your only involvement in this activity is to source the game for them to play, give them the opportunity to do it, and support them to overcome any issues they encounter.

Problem: Workload

I have yet to meet a teacher whose work week equates to our contracted hours. Many of us go in to work early to set up our classrooms and prepare work for the day ahead. We often take work home to mark or spend evenings or weekends planning and evaluating for our learners. Some manage a work-life balance, but many don't. Adding something else to the workload is not going to be met kindly!

With the amount of planning and marking required to meet pupils' needs and create next steps for them, not to mention providing them with feedback, completing data paperwork, monitoring, and tracking, there is little chance of an opportunity to set up Tuff Trays or spend time creating or looking up different activities that will challenge them sufficiently.

Solution

The workload of a teacher does seem endless. There's always planning, marking, organising, resourcing, or meetings to be done. My intention when writing this book was not to introduce something to add to this list. On the contrary, play can provide an opportunity for a deep breath for teachers. Consider the Monopoly example – allowing your learners the opportunity to play some carefully selected board games gives them a chance to develop skills in a relaxed way and gives you a chance to observe your class, their interactions, and their application of skills. Once your play-based or contextualised, classroom is set up, offering pupils the opportunity to play and put their learning into practice gives you the opportunity to observe them, engage them in conversation, listen to their conversations with each other, and just enjoy spending time with them. I have personally found the introduction of this style of teaching into my classroom to be invigorating and allows me to see how well a concept has been understood by my learners. A textbook page on money shows me how much they understand the abstract concept, but observing them make shopping lists, browse catalogues, compare prices, calculate totals and change, and discuss whether to use their credit or debit card shows a different level of understanding that I can evidence through simple observation sheets or lesson evaluations.

Problem: Behaviour

Surely if I just let the class play, behaviour will become unmanageable? Behaviour management can be a struggle at the best of times, and play-based learning means giving up control. Won't that inevitably lead to poorer behaviour, class disruption, and incompletion of work tasks?

Solution

Every child and every classroom is different, but what has surprised me about developing this pedagogy is that empowering children and giving them some ownership in their learning can actually lead to an improvement in behaviour. Learning that is more enjoyable leads to better engagement, and engaged learners stay on task. Not to mention, giving your learners options, asking them for their opinions and feedback, and spending time with them all help build confidence and self-esteem. I can't emphasise this enough; a play-based approach does not mean allowing your students to play all day, every day. It is an approach to learning that allows them to apply what you teach them in a context that means something to them. It allows them to engage in learning that interests them, to apply their learning, to work alone, to work with others, and to find a way to understand more deeply the things that we want them to learn. And to do this in a safe, supportive, and encouraging environment. We do what we can to support our learners, and hopefully, they will work along with us to look for better ways to achieve their goals.

These solution-focussed approaches paint a rosy view of introducing the play principles to your teaching. It is worth reiterating that with any teaching style, teachers need to consider what works for their learners, their setting, and what works for them. There are ways to introduce elements of contextualised learning to your class without going all in. Some real-life examples of practice will be shared later in this book, and I would encourage you to reflect on your own practice, your own personality, and your own school and class (or classes) to pick out the elements that might work for you.

Take Away

We teachers are very busy people with more and more being piled onto our plates. With attainment scores, mounting workload, time constraints, behaviour management, and a packed curriculum, there is no shortage of reasons not to introduce something new.

But let's not look at play as an additional add-on. We can look at it as an alternative that might actually help with some of these other issues.

The purpose of this book is not to add to your workload – quite the opposite, in fact. If we look as play as something that might help us teach and will definitely help our students learn, then it has to be a positive change.

6 Record Keeping

As with pretty much everything in education, there needs to be evidence to show that your approach is making a positive impact on the education of your learners. Depending on your reasons for introducing a more play-based approach, this evidence can take a range of forms.

Evidence can help back up your new approach and reassure you that it is supporting your learners. If it is not, then you need to make changes! Be prepared to be flexible – what works for one Primary 6 (or Year 5) class won't necessarily work for all classes. It might not even work for another Primary 6 (or Year 5) class.

If you are lucky enough to have a Senior Leadership or Management Team that supports your innovative approaches, you will be allowed a certain amount of time to implement your changes and tweak any issues – but there will need to be positive results before too long!

As a teacher, you will already plan your next steps, give your learners feedback, and engage in a dialogue about their learning. This is all still the case when engaging in play activities. You will provide feedback to parents through whichever means your school uses, and you will evaluate your teaching and resources, including the learning space. None of this changes when you apply a play-based approach.

Traditional written work can be marked, assessed, and graded, which can give a fairly clear picture of how a learner is progressing through the curriculum and outcomes or standards. What is less clear is how that learner is progressing in a more holistic sense, linking curricular areas emotionally and socially and applying their learning in real contexts.

There is a variety of ways you can measure the impact of your play-based approach. You will have assessments that you would routinely do in your school that will show any increase in attainment, and hopefully, your new approach will be reflected in this.

In any classroom, the pupils themselves are the best evidence available of the progress they are making. A conversation with their teacher will tell you where they have come from and how far they have come, their strengths, their development areas, and what their main passions and interests are. This, however, is often not evidence enough, and we are asked to provide test scores and paperwork to back up any professional opinion we have. You can keep a record of the work you and the class have done and keep a note of the impact and learning that has taken place. Alternatively, you can plan for your play-based approach as an intervention to address a particular issue, for example, increasing engagement or deepening understanding and recall. You can then record how you plan to carry this out and what the outcomes are.

DOI: 10.4324/9781003486602-8

Record Keeping 39

Your own school or council/district may have its own methods of recording that you can access and adapt to suit your needs, and I would always suggest investigating this before choosing your own method of recording data. For example, there may be a method of recording, commonly used in the early years, that can be adapted to reflect the work being done in the more senior classes, or a local school that has a method they could share and support you with.

If this is not available to you, the following are some suggestions of methods of recording you might consider.

Record of Work

These methods are intended to record what you have done and what happened. They are not plans and are responsive but can link to planned learning.

Reflection Book or Floor Book

A book can be updated daily or weekly to keep a record of activities, lessons, and learning, as well as reactions from the learners, photos and/or observations of additional learning. It is important to consider the purpose of a book like this – is it simply to keep a record of what you (the teacher) are doing, or is it for the learners to add to, read over, and reflect on as well? I keep a class record of our weekly learning. Every Friday, we reflect on our key learning

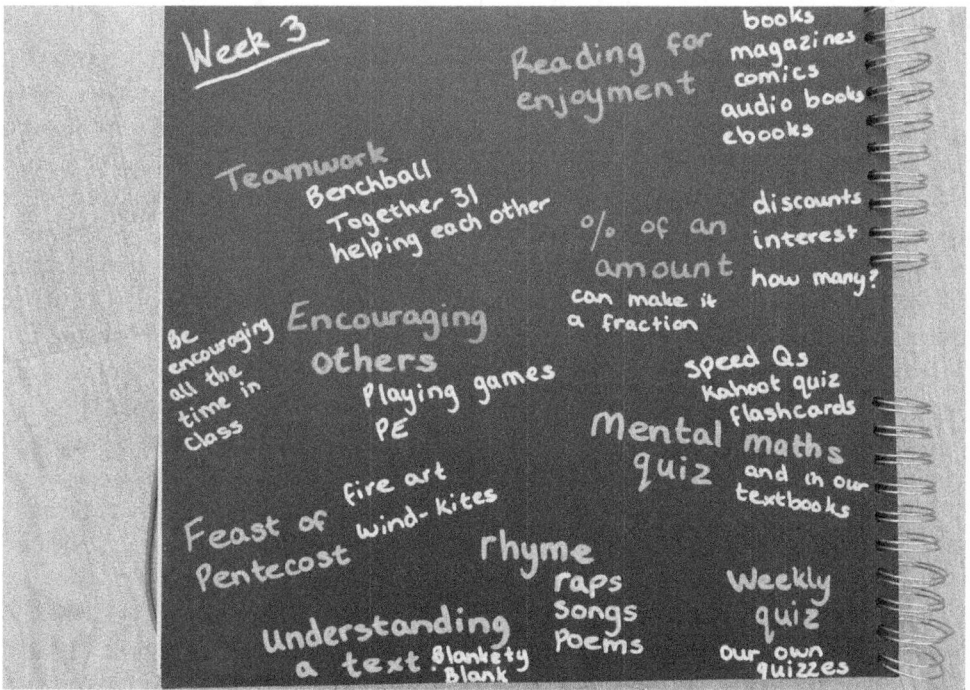

Figure 6.1 Reflection Book

activities from the week and write about them in our book. The pupils then get to pick something from the book to work on independently for a while on a Friday afternoon. Apart from being a time for learners to engage in something they enjoy and choose to do, I also have a record of what they have remembered from their learning and verbal feedback on how they have felt about it. It gives me just as much of an opportunity to reflect as the learners.

If the play approach is designed to support a specific learner (or small group of learners), a journal might be the best way to record progress. The journal could contain photos, quotes, pieces of work, and any assessment results to provide a more rounded account of the progress the child or children have made. As we know, assessment results do not always tell the full story.

Pupil Records

You could have your learners keep their own record of their learning, either individually or in groups. This could be in the form of floor books, as mentioned previously, or it could be a class magazine, podcasts, or a class blog. You could give them some guidance as to topics to cover – what are you improving on, what I still need to work on, etc. – but allow them the freedom to give honest and personal responses in their chosen way.

Observations

In the early years, play is often measured through observations. Observations can be invaluable in recording how pupils engage in their play activities and the direction they take. In the upper stages, however, more emphasis is placed on attainment and formal assessments, so while observations will be a good indicator of how learners engage with their activities, it might be more beneficial to also measure how this is transferring to other areas of their learning. One way to do this is to use something like a Meta Skills Progression Framework (Skills Development Scotland – link in References Section) to record the development of skills. You can track the class as a whole – how are they accessing the areas? What are they doing? Who is working with who? Or you can make observations of areas and resources – How are the resources being used? What are they being used for? Are any being used more than others? Or you can select targeted learners, those you are trying to engage more, support behaviour, or raise attainment – observe their interactions, ask questions, note their answers, listen to their conversations, monitor how they transfer their skills into other areas. If you have little or no support in the classroom, be creative with how you observe learning through play. Observe targeted pupils only or occasionally ask pupils for feedback or to give peer feedback.

Observations can be a formal or informal method of recording the impact and results of play. If you choose to use a formal method, you will need links to the curriculum, attainment results, and pupil feedback, as well as your own subjective view of what you see.

Informal observations can be more personal and, quite often, are more reflective of the whole learner, as they demonstrate their personal progress and development in reference to where they have come from rather than compared to national standards or others in the class.

Pupil Feedback

One of the most valuable pieces of feedback for me has been from the pupils themselves. Hearing them be excited about their learning or say they are looking forward to coming in each morning makes my job a whole lot easier. There are pupils in my current class who previously recorded low engagement in their learning who now look forward to a Monday morning to see what the new Tuff Tray challenge is for the week. You can do this by noting their comments, having a vocal recording of their feedback, or even videoing them, if permitted. If you have a way to record the pupils' responses and feedback to your approach, you have evidence.

Celebrate the Successes

We can record pupil feedback formally so that we have records, but I often ask pupils to share what they have been learning or send them to the Senior Management Team with a piece of their work created during a contextualised play activity. It helps reinforce to management that they are learning while they play, but it also instils some pride in the pupils about their play. Their independent learning becomes more directed and purposeful as learners develop their skills and transfer what they have learned through our teaching as well as their own investigating. Have a class success book or share photos on a platform that your school is happy using and encourage your pupils to talk about their learning in a positive but educational way. "We played with the toy money today" doesn't sound as good as "we role played shops where we had to stick to a budget, and I was only allowed to use my debit card for £30 of my shopping"!

Planned Interventions

You may be implementing a play-based approach to target something specific like attendance, late-coming, or engagement. If you are planning an intervention like this, an APDR (Assess, Plan, Do, Review) or PDSA (Plan, Do, Study, Act) would be a good way to record the proposed change and its effects.

To measure the specific impact of play and a play-based approach, there are alternative measurements you may need to take. Measuring test scores or attendance data lends itself nicely to recording change – if test scores go up or attendance improves, then things are going well. If you are looking to measure more subjective areas such as engagement, involvement, or application, you will need some kind of scale to measure against. You can simply use a traffic light system (green = engaged; orange = 50/50; red = not engaged), or you can use a more detailed measuring scale. You will need to have a starting point, so it is a good idea to take a baseline measure – how engaged are your class or learner before you introduce your play-based approach?

One scale that is often used as a measurement tool for play activities is the Leuven 5-point Scale (Barber, 2013). It can be used to measure a learner's involvement in an activity.

This scale can be particularly useful for measuring engagement and involvement in play activities, but it focuses less on learning and depends on observations, which can be

Table 6.1 The Leuven Scale for Involvement

Level	Well-being	Signals
1	Extremely Low	Activity is simple, repetitive, and passive. The child seems absent and displays no energy. They may stare into space or look around to see what others are doing.
2	Low	Frequently interrupted activity. The child will be engaged in the activity for some of the time they are observed, but there will be moments of non-activity when they will stare into space or be distracted by what is going on around them.
3	Moderate	Mainly continuous activity. The child is busy with the activity but at a fairly routine level, and there are few signs of real involvement. They make some progress with what they are doing but don't show much energy and concentration and can be easily distracted.
4	High	Continuous activity with intense movements. The child's activity has intense moments, and, at all times, they seem involved. They are not easily distracted.
5	Extremely High	The child shows continuous and intense activity, revealing the greatest involvement. They are concentrated, creative, energetic, and persistent throughout nearly all the observed periods.

Table 6.2 The Simpson Engagement Scale

6	Listened to input, started activity, and completed all/almost all (over 90%) of the task independently – with or without stuck strategies.
5	Listened to input, completed most (75-90%) of task using agreed strategies independently.
4	Listened to input, started, and completed all/almost all of task (over 90%) with support.
3	Listened to input, completed the majority (50-74%) of task with support.
2	Listened to input, completed less than half (15-49%) of task.
1	In room but unable or unwilling to access support. Less than 15% of task completed.
0	Disengaged from lesson, refused to enter room, or exited room. Refused to access support. No work completed.

subjective. In the Upper Stages, we may wish to measure engagement in a specific, given task, so failing to find something that met my needs, I created my own scales of measurement.

In my Support for Learning role a few years ago, I worked with teachers and other colleagues to create methods of measuring the impact of supportive interventions, including measuring engagement before attempting to increase attainment. I wanted something that specifically measured engagement in learning. Through this, I developed an Engagement Scale (see Table 6.2), which I unashamedly and unoriginally named after myself and have used effectively to show changes in pupil engagement in their learning. I have since developed this to be more in line with HMIe (His Majesty's Inspectorate of Education) measures and now use it to measure the engagement of targeted individuals in my class who have previously struggled to engage with their learning.

Following the use of my Engagement Scale, I then developed an Attainment Scale (see Table 6.3), using similar HMIe-related levels to measure achieved attainment levels in any given lesson. While these are not yet widely recognised measurement scales, I am providing them as examples. If a specific measurement tool does not exist for what you are looking to measure, or you can't find a tool you need, sometimes you have to be innovative and create your own!

Table 6.3 The Simpson Attainment Scale

5	All or almost all of task was completed accurately (over 90% of Success Criteria met).
4	Most of task was completed accurately (75-90% of Success Criteria met).
3	Majority of task was completed accurately (50-74% of Success Criteria met).
2	Less than half of the task was completed accurately (15-49% of Success Criteria met).
1	Hardly any of task was completed accurately (Less than 15% of the Success Criteria met).

Action Research

Measuring can be carried out in cycles either using an APDR (Assess, Plan, Do, Review) or a PDSA (Plan, Do, Study, Act). Examples of each of these can be found in the Appendix section.

A record of the impact of your change, such as an APDR (Assess, Plan, Do, Review) or PDSA (Plan, Do, Study, Act), would be useful in providing details of what was happening, the issue, what you wanted to change, how you changed it, and what the measurable impact was.

These allow us to regularly reflect on our play pedagogy and adjust according to feedback from the learners. If they are not engaging with certain areas or resources, struggling to transition from play to more formal learning, or not using the resources in the way you had hoped to extend their learning, change it. The APDR or PDSA allows you to have a record of what you have tried, what has worked, and what has needed to be tweaked. It shows you are continually reflecting on your practise and making changes accordingly.

Ultimately, the proof will be in the pudding. Any standardised assessments should show the impact of your teaching pedagogy. The whole point of a more play-based, contextualised approach is to give your learners the skills, tools, and independence they need to deepen their understanding and transfer their knowledge more effectively.

Take Away

Record the impact of your approach. Attainment data will always show how learners are progressing academically, but it does not necessarily tell the whole story.

An effective play-based approach will result in increased attainment data, but it is also good to have a record of any improvements in engagement, social interactions, skill development, application of learning in contexts, or even attendance to show the impact of your approach.

References

Barber, J. (2013). Leuven Wellbeing Scales. *Early Years Educator* 15(6). https://doi.org/10.12968/eyed.2013.15.6.32

Skills Development Scotland - Meta Skills Framework. www.skillsdevelopmentscotland.co.uk/what-we-do/scotlands-careers-services/education-team/meta-skills-toolkit

SECTION 2
Putting it into Practice

7 Setting the Scene

Classroom Layout

The way we set up our classrooms sets the scene for the year ahead. How we welcome learners to our room and how they feel about the classroom going forward plays a huge role in how they feel about learning, as well as their motivation and effort. How many of us set up our classrooms the way we like them and hope the learners will simply fit in?

These days, I try to find out as much as I can about the learners I am about to take on and set up my classroom in a way that meets the initial needs of the class, as well as reflecting me and my style of teaching.

If you can involve your learners in the organising of your classroom, this helps create a child-led, playful environment. By asking for their input and, more importantly, listening to it, you allow pupils to feel like it is *their* classroom rather than your classroom that they come to spend some time in. Having a classroom that they feel part of and that meets their needs will help support their learning in so many ways.

If you are lucky enough to have a large, spacious classroom, there is plenty of scope for creating areas for play opportunities. As in infant classrooms, it is great if you can have dedicated areas for construction, role play, small world, and creativity or art activities. If you don't have this luxury, there are other ways you can offer your learners opportunities to play but in a more confined manner. And let's be honest, in an upper-stage classroom, with bigger furniture and pupils, there usually isn't a lot of space, but you can be clever with how you arrange your resources.

Classroom Organisation

An organised and playful classroom lets your learners know that learning is going to be fun, consistent, engaging, it's going to have opportunities, and it's going to involve them.

Continuous provision, as described in Chapter 1, should be freely available to learners and remain constant throughout the year. Your classroom should, therefore, be set up with consistent resources available for play and exploration. The play opportunities can be available openly, laid out on dedicated tables or Tuff Trays, or displayed as part of your Numeracy or Literacy areas. When the learners are older, it might be more appropriate to have your resources in baskets in units, boxes on the windowsill, or trays that they can access

48 *Putting it into Practice*

Figure 7.1 Cleaning Resources

independently. Label your containers clearly so all learners and visitors to the classroom know what is in each box or tray.

Once it is set up, there shouldn't be much change required.

Have areas of the classroom that provide contextual opportunities without explicitly being for play. As learners grow and mature, their play changes. They can play with calculators, storyboards, puzzles, or measuring tapes. I have had a cleaning station in my classroom, complete with cloths, washing up liquid, spray bottles, and a dustpan and brush, as members of the class would regularly ask if they could clean and tidy. We even regularly borrow the cleaner's vacuum cleaner to 'play' at cleaning the classroom!

So, let's look at the different areas of the classroom and how we might arrange our environment to maximise playful opportunities within them without completely renovating our classrooms.

Seating Arrangements

I usually start each year by allowing my class to choose where they sit. Inevitably, I need to rearrange the seating within the first week or so, but I explain clearly that this is due to how the arrangements affected their work. It doesn't do anyone any good sitting next to someone who distracts them, or they frequently fall out with, or who doesn't help them as much as someone else could. By giving them a choice at the beginning, you are demonstrating that you are willing to try their suggestions. If and when they don't work successfully, calmly explain that it was worth giving it a shot, but maybe next year you will be ready to sit together!

We have 'Home Seats', a base where learners start each day. These are usually our seats for Numeracy and Literacy as well – seats where I know we are catering to the learners who need space, who need to be near the board, who need to be near a supportive peer, or need to be near specific resources. With some P7 (Year 6) classes, in the final term, I have had the learners move seats for every lesson – they have their Numeracy seats, Literacy seats, Science seats, etc. I do this for several reasons, all in preparation for high school: getting pupils used to working with different peers, getting used to sitting in different areas of the classroom, and getting used to not having your own seat. This strategy doesn't work for every class, so consider your class as a whole as well as individual learners who may have learning needs that mean moving seats would be detrimental to their learning. Generally, it is beneficial to organise your seating arrangements early on and not deviate from them too much. Listen to your learners, though – they may be telling you through their words or behaviours that a previously effective seat is no longer working for them.

At other times, I engage in some alternative seating arrangements. Musical chairs, where the class walks around while music plays. When the music stops, learners must sit in the nearest available seat, and this is where they will complete a given task. I sometimes need to do this a couple of times to really shake up the classroom! We have also had 'extreme' reading/writing/numeracy lessons, where we complete a short task in an unusual position – under tables, upside down in chairs, standing on one leg!

In the warmer months, the option to take your learning outdoors is always attractive and should be considered. We occasionally also have timed activities where stations are set up around the room where groups try to complete a task in a given time before we all move around to the next station. It's a bit like speed dating but speed numeracy activities instead!

These fun suggestions will probably only be suitable for short, individual tasks. Longer term, more consideration may be needed for seating conducive to effective learning and that learners' needs are being met.

Reading/Writing Areas – Most upper stages classrooms will already have a library or reading area. Why not add some paper and writing materials to the area to add an extra level of creativity? Different pens, blank jotters, and templates.

And, if you can, mix up your reading materials – books (picture books, short novels, more advanced novels, graphic novels), comics, magazines, and newspapers. If you have access to the technology, audiobooks and eBooks are a great alternative for reluctant readers. Give your learners some choice. Allow them some exploration and hopefully the discovery of something that grabs their interests. Remember, it is not about giving yourself more to do, it is just giving the pupils more scope to be creative and play with resources they already have and opportunities to practice what we have been teaching them freely.

Maths/Numeracy – Again, you probably already have a Numeracy area or at least a wall display. While an infant classroom might have a Tuff Tray with a range of materials for number activities, we can have a table of numeracy games, a tray of maths equipment (measuring tapes, timers, calculators, etc.), or even a couple of poly pockets stuck to the wall with a fun challenge or games to try. Try to always have number activities available, but tailor the resources to whatever you are currently teaching to allow opportunities for independent

50   *Putting it into Practice*

Figure 7.2 Reading Resources

exploration and application. When teaching money, have some catalogues, play money, and a till. When teaching measure, have some scales, tape measures, and rulers in an accessible place.

If you have the space, try to have some resources related to every area available somewhere to allow retrieval and revisiting to take place. Even when you are not explicitly learning about money, leaving some play money out all year allows pupils to revisit it and link it to other areas. Some work on percentages might encourage a bit of role-play with a 25% sale! What I try to do is keep the items on the Numeracy table linked to what we are learning about at the time but keep other items available in trays for the pupils to access independently whenever they need to. These materials can support learners in progressing from the concrete concepts of mathematics (manipulating physical materials) to the pictorial (textbooks or workbooks), then to the abstract and application of concepts to real-life contexts in order to deepen understanding.

You may also want to have a selection of numeracy games available for the class to access as an alternative learning activity or to consolidate learning. We all know that the repetition of an action or activity deepens understanding, but variety in how we repeat it supports engagement, so games and alternative activities are a vital accompaniment to textbook and written work.

You might also want to consider having a way of storing the resources you frequently use for other play-based lessons. I have a wheeled trolley stand that holds six trays. I use it for craft materials, junk, whiteboards, chalk pens, etc., and I can wheel it out whenever I need it for a certain lesson. By having playful resources and play-based learning consistently in your

Setting the Scene 51

Figure 7.3 Numeracy Resources

classroom, the concept of play as a treat or an extra wears off. Pupils are secure and reassured about the presence of play in their classrooms; it becomes part of their learning and not something they are seeking or fighting for.

Take Away

Set your classroom up to reflect your play-based approach. Have resources available that the learners can access independently when they need to explore, investigate, or research something that interests them. Have resources linked to your teaching so that learners can extend their learning and perhaps apply it in their own contexts to deepen their understanding. Plan and organise your classroom with your class in mind, but also with them if you can.

8 Resources

This chapter will give you some ideas for resources you can have in your classroom to support and enhance your play-based approach. There will be many resources you already have in your classroom and perhaps some alternative uses for old favourites.

I never advocate for teachers spending their own money on classroom resources, but if you are looking to buy, please search out charity shops or opportunities on social media to obtain resources free or at a very low price.

Apart from the interests of your learners, resourcing the play in your classroom will depend on a number of things: mainly available space, available funds, and available support.

In an ideal world, we would all have space for different dedicated contextual areas, with money available for lots of new resources and at least one additional adult to help with observations and facilitating play with those who need support.

If space is limited, a tray unit can house all the different resources you need. If funding is tight, have a rummage through school cupboards. Most of my resources have been dug out of the back of colleagues' cupboards or long-forgotten resources from years gone by. I go with the theory that if it's covered in dust, it's up for grabs!

It is generally agreed that there are certain resources that are well suited to meeting the developmental needs of learners through play. While this tends to refer to those in the early years, it can easily be adapted to be more appropriate for older learners. By providing challenges or questions, you can push your learners to extend their learning using these resources, whether they are left out all the time or stored in trays or boxes with their accompanying challenge cards.

What follows are some of the most regularly recommended resources for classroom play, along with some ideas on how to adapt them for older learners. I have also provided some suggestions for challenges or questions you can pose to your pupils alongside these resources to encourage their learning progression.

Small World - Traditionally, this might be a dolls' house with dolls or miniature characters for children to manipulate in whatever way helps them make sense of the world. This can simply be a box or tray with miniature characters and some furniture. All learners need opportunities to make sense of the world around them, and small world manipulation is a great way to do this. The characters do not have to be elaborate; I have seen children act out scenarios with chess pieces!

Figure 8.1 Duplo Characters

Suggested challenges:

- Create names and personality descriptions for our tiny people.
- What is the back story/origin story of our tiny people?
- Create a dramatic/scary/problem-solving story involving our tiny people.
- Once upon a time, the tiny people were out for a walk. It was a beautiful, calm day when all of a sudden . . .

Home Corner – In the early years classroom, this might be a small kitchen area with various resources for playing house. Again, this is another opportunity for learners to make sense of their world in a safe space. But this can just as easily be a box or tray of items that can be used in a similar way – a phone, cups, plates, baby doll, and saucepan have been enough for my class to create a whole story about family life. I have seen learners use these resources for role play about the world of work rather than family life, so I will often include an old office phone, computer keyboard, and notepad as well.

Suggested challenges:

- What kind of a home would you like to live in?
- What does family life look like?
- It's a tough job, but someone's got to do it – what job are you doing?

54 Putting it into Practice

Construction – This would traditionally include wooden blocks in a younger classroom, but they can be Lego, Kapla, K*Nex, or any other materials the pupils can build creatively with. You can keep a box of this stuff under a table, on a windowsill, or just in a tray in a tray unit. If you are so inclined, you can provide challenge cards or make themed activities for them. Or not. Providing the resources for learners to be creative is enough.

Suggested challenges:

- Build a home for a hamster/fairy/tiny witch.
- Design a modern tower to rival the Burj Khalifa.
- Can you build a bridge from A to B that can hold two cars?

Cars/Vehicles – You don't need a garage or road map on the floor for this to be useful. A small box or tub of cars and other vehicles will do, but if you have a bit more space, a roadmap or junk that could be used to create a landscape is great. This resource can be very useful for STEM activities involving speed, distance, and time or angles involving ramps.

Suggested challenges:

- Can you create a car park where all of the cars can park with enough space to drive in/out?
- Design a road system for the cars to get around.
- The cars need a multi-storey garage.

Figure 8.2 Toy Cars

Art – Opportunities to be creative and artistic without teacher input are rare in the upper stages classroom. Though it can be very tricky to find space for a designated art area, even just storing your art resources somewhere that the pupils have access to can be enough. If you feel it's appropriate, allow your learners the option of choosing an arty activity when they are finished with their non-negotiable task or at the end of the week. Particularly those learners for whom traditional tasks involving reading and writing can be tiring. Perhaps use your judgement on the time needed to tidy up and which materials should be available. Pencils, crayons, and paper all the time; paint and glitter only when you have the energy for them!

Suggested challenges (I would leave these deliberately vague – let them be creative):

- Design
- Colours that go well together
- Pattern

Games

When it comes to games that allow learners to apply a specific concept or practise a certain skill, you might need to be creative. Adapt resources you already have to make those that encourage a playful and contextual approach to learning as well as allow learners an opportunity to develop their skills and apply their learning. I have used the following ideas with some success, and these might be a good place to start:

- Headbandz –This game can be used to develop conversation, listening, and describing skills just as it is. By creating new cards for the headbands, you can create a way to describe concepts that you have been teaching. Cards that feature mathematical concepts or parts of the body will give your pupils the challenge of describing something they have been learning about as well as the language that accompanies it and describing it to others – which is always helpful when you need pupils to explain what they have been learning about to others!
- Guess Who – There are many variations of this game around, but the concept is the same: ask questions to work out which character your opponent has. Played as it is, it can be used to develop descriptive language, and you can give specific challenges, such as using adjectives or similes to describe the character. Alternatively, you could allocate careers to each character, and each player has to work out the job of their opponent's character. Or allocate them famous events, numbers, or even chemical elements! If you have the time (or inclination), you could also change the character cards to famous historical figures. Or healthy foods. Or important landmarks.
- Dice – For addition of 3, 4, or 5 numbers or multiplication up to 6 × 6. I have also created a bank of six topics, sentence starts, or challenges and the dice determine the task. Differently numbered dice can be used in place value, chance, or probability activities.
- Uno – These cards are great for place value activities, creating 5-, 6-, and 7-digit numbers and rearranging to create smaller numbers or discuss the impact of changing the digit in a specific place. Dealing a certain number of the cards out and making

56 *Putting it into Practice*

Figure 8.3 Uno Cards

the biggest (or smallest) number you can. There's a lot more that you can use these number cards for, and I'm sure the children will come up with some!

Take Away

Do not spend a lot of money on resources unless you have been given funds to do so! Children will use their imaginations and play with any resources you provide.

Recommended resources include those that help learners make sense of the world around them – so dolls, house items, cars, and building materials.

Use your own imagination to add challenges or curricular links to games you already have to provide your learners with opportunities to consolidate their learning in a fun and engaging way.

9 Creating a Playful Ethos

Incorporating Play into your Timetable

As mentioned previously, there is a field of theory that all children should be given time for free play throughout their education. If you are able to facilitate this during your classroom time, then you should. The class will definitely benefit from this, and it might be exactly what the learners in your class need. However, how much time you can and should dedicate to truly free play will depend very much on your circumstances. Scheduling regular play opportunities into your timetable might be next to impossible. It certainly has been very difficult for me. In my current class, I put aside a session in the first week of term to discuss the meaning of play and contextualised learning for us and explained my target of raising their attainment alongside their desire to enjoy their learning. We agreed as a class on how to set up the classroom and how to resource our Play Trays so there would always be an element of play in the classroom. See Chapter 16 for more on continuous provision.

As a teacher with attainment targets to reach, children to motivate, and a whole class to manage, however, I find this type of play on a large scale quite impractical in a busy classroom with a curriculum to cover. I also feel it would be somewhat irresponsible of me to give my students the idea that this is a form of learning they can expect as they progress onto high school and further education. Part of my job is to prepare my learners for the next stage of their learning. As an upper-stage teacher, I need to help them develop skills that they can transfer into all of their learning while also giving them a realistic expectation of how this will look for them. Through playful learning and play-based activities, I can teach them how to be more intrinsically motivated and personally driven and hopefully fully embrace learning opportunities. However, completely free play, which is without adult intervention and instruction, is not something they will experience a lot in high school, and I need to prepare them for that.

Saying that, I do ensure that there is time for play in our week, and I encourage the class to use their breaks and lunchtimes for free play by discussing activities they can do, allowing them to borrow equipment to bring outside, and teaching them games they can play independently.

So, how do we bring play into our classrooms while still guiding the teaching and learning? What I believe it boils down to is our role in the classroom and how play can fit in. I would like you to take a moment to reflect on what you consider to be your role in your own classroom.

If it is to teach. To control your class. To pass on knowledge, to teach skills, and to help students retain enough information to pass their next standardised assessment, then a fully play-based approach probably isn't for you. No judgement here, just reality and reflection on our own preferred way of teaching. A play-based approach is much more learner-led, more flexible, more holistic than just paper-based assessments, and much less in the control of the teacher. That type of approach isn't for everyone.

If you feel that your role is more to facilitate, to encourage, to support, and to inspire, then this might well be the approach for you. One of my favourite teacher quotes is, "The best teachers are those who show you where to look but don't tell you what to see" (Alexandra K. Trenfor). I have it stuck beside my desk to remind me that it is not my job to tell my students everything they need to know. It is my job to help them uncover, find out, and learn through experience as much, if not more, than the imparting of facts and information.

There is no right or wrong approach to this, only what works best for you and your learners. Teachers all have their own interpretation of what play means, how it might be applied in their classroom, and what their role will be, and this will differ among us all. Whatever works in your situation is the right move. But we must remember that we are not the all-knowing experts whose job is simply to impart information for our students to absorb. We need to provide them with experiences and opportunities to learn in different ways. You will know (or be on a journey to discover) the way that works best for you.

What I have found is that, in practice, there is no one-size-fits-all approach to implementing play in your classroom. I know that is not a revelation to you, as that is true of every teaching and learning approach out there. It is all about getting to know your class, knowing yourself as a teacher, and working out what works best for all of you. For some teachers, the full-on play aspect is what excites them, involving the students and allowing them to lead their own learning all the time. For others, the loss of control terrifies them, so bringing in small elements of play into their traditional practice is easier to manage.

For me, I am somewhere in between. I involve pupils in leading their own learning as much as I can, but I still teach traditionally before giving the class time and opportunities to apply and develop newly learned concepts and knowledge. I have seen a huge improvement in students' awareness of their own attainment levels and progress as well as in engagement and motivation. I have also seen improvements in interest in what they are learning, wonder, fascination, and connections to their own lives, and that, for me, is what a play-based or contextual approach is all about.

Pedagogy

I usually start my new session with my new class by talking to them about their perceptions of learning and play. We then work together to discuss how we can learn through contextualised opportunities and how we can incorporate this into our week. I often need to revisit this discussion, especially after a particularly fun lesson, to remind pupils what they are learning. There can be a struggle with the transition from the 'new' way back to the 'old' way. If you have a balance where you sometimes teach traditionally with textbooks or work from the board and other times allow pupils to lead and play, there will be some who want one method but not the other. I explain it to my class with the term, 'non-negotiable tasks'. These are tasks that must be completed (or at least reasonably attempted) and that won't go away. If not completed to an acceptable standard (and this will vary between learners), they must be completed at another time, usually during a more playful time. It's all about the balance.

As mentioned previously, in preparing our learners for their secondary education, it would be ill-advised to throw out our traditional way of teaching and completely replace it with play or contextualised opportunities. Play is freely chosen and intrinsically motivated, and we all know some pupils who would never choose textbook or jotter work and would not be motivated to challenge themselves to advance through the benchmarks or standards.

For this reason, in my own practice, I still teach using Learning Intentions and Success Criteria (in line with my school policy) followed by a non-negotiable task, whether it be a textbook page, a written task, or the creation of something. Once this is completed, pupils may have some choice in their follow-up task to apply their learning in different ways. Where appropriate, I also allow some flexibility in how their non-negotiable task is completed, such as recording answers, seating arrangements, writing implements, or partner support. I then link the available games or activities to the learning we have been doing where possible.

If you can timetable opportunities for play and it works for your class, then that's great. What I have found useful for my classes is developing a timetable that reassures them that the more play-based lessons and opportunities are consistent as well as having opportunities in the classroom, such as a Tuff Tray, that are always available to them when they need them.

Typically, I timetable my week with more conceptual and theoretical learning at the start of the week – a numeracy skill followed by a textbook page or a lesson on a focussed writing skill with a specific writing task. Later in the week, I schedule more contextualised lessons and opportunities for pupils to apply their learning. This might take the form of some numeracy stations, a problem-solving challenge, or a writing lesson focused on a real-life situation we are facing, such as scripting our assembly or writing to local businesses for donations for a fundraiser.

To illustrate, my Monday mornings are usually for conceptual Numeracy work – such as textbooks, abstract calculations, and theory. Tuesdays are for word problems linked to Monday's work and problem-solving using real-life examples. Wednesday and Thursday, I revisit the conceptual aspects with a quiz and challenge them to apply it in a STEM challenge or a real-life application. This is quite often part of a project-based approach that we build on each week, adding more challenges each time – such as percentage work linking to calculating interest from the bank or shares in a business. Fridays tend to be a check-in on understanding, usually through activity stations. The stations will involve independent activities; while at one of the stations, I ask questions and check the depth of understanding. This approach means that I am meeting the learning styles of as many learners as possible – some prefer the textbooks, some prefer the context of word problems, and some prefer the more hands-on application. As for the continuous provision, most of my learners like to access the tray resources once they have completed their 'non-negotiable' task if there is time, but some need to use the opportunities for breaks in their learning. As the term goes on, I find even my learners who struggle to engage in a full lesson will engage with the contextual learning resources as a means of taking a break. For me, this is an improvement in brain breaks that can see them removed from the classroom environment and their peers. It is worth mentioning, though, that, of course, there are pupils who may need to have their break outside of the room or even outside of the school building, but in the main, keeping learners included in their own class is preferred.

Keep a playful approach in mind when you are thinking about delivering your curricular learning. This is creatively about how you can bring play into the lessons you already teach. It is not about reinventing the wheel; it is about being flexible in your approach and making learning fun and engaging as well as challenging for your learners.

Writing

Once a week, I provide a slot for free writing. We call it Free Write Fridays (original, I know!), and in that half hour or so, pupils can write about anything they want (topic) in any style they want (story, newspaper article, comic strip) with anything they want (pen, pencil, crayon, laptop) and on anything they want (lined paper, giant paper, jotter, PowerPoint, Word). The results are always varied and very interesting, but it provides a stress-free writing experience for the learners that they know I will read and give formative feedback on, but not correct. I do use these pieces to inform my next steps in teaching and support, though.

I also provide a range of writing materials on the Literacy table for learners to access when they need to, such as blank jotters (half lined, half blank is great so they can illustrate their writing), blank comic strips, pens, coloured paper – whatever you can find in the cupboards! There are also some spelling and word games, such as Scrabble and Sentence Scramble, to allow opportunities for word practise.

Figure 9.1 Letter Tiles

Reading

My reading corner has been designed and set up by my pupils. It is their reading area, and I want them to have ownership of it. We start each term by discussing the reading materials available to them. What books are they into? What authors do they want to include? What alternative materials do they want? It is regularly updated, and as learners' interests and preferences change, so do the books in our library. Giving a choice means allowing exploration and the hopeful discovery of something that interests them. The main principle of play is choice, and if we are considering reading in a real-world context, we read for two main purposes – for information and for enjoyment. The enjoyment of reading comes from reading something you choose. When reading for pleasure, I don't ever tell children they have to complete a book they are not enjoying. As an adult, if I am not enjoying a book, I probably won't finish it. I will change it to something I want to read instead. This is ok for children, too.

When reading for information, on the other hand, I try to make this link to a context that makes sense to my pupils by finding out information that they will then use for other purpose. Or read instructions to create something or complete something. Abstract texts with accompanying questions are our usual way to uncover a pupil's understanding of a text, but would it be more useful to them if it was more real for them? There is a valuable place for reading an unfamiliar text and answering questions to determine comprehension, and the simplest way to make this relevant is to change the names of any characters or places to those with whom they are familiar. I have seen it make a surprising difference in a child's understanding of the text they have read.

Numeracy and Maths

Learners need formal numeracy and mathematical lessons to be taught new concepts, and they need time to build on that new knowledge during play-based activities. The balance between the two is crucial. The opportunity to play allows pupils to revisit concepts regularly and apply them in different contexts. The time to play with peers also allows for discussions and explanations between each other that can deepen understanding in a way that teacher input never could. Concentrating only on teaching the traditional curriculum misses the opportunity to challenge those who have a firm grasp of the concepts being taught and support those who need an alternative method of learning. Play-based learning in mathematics is more fun and meets the needs of all children (Vogt et al., 2018).

When I stand at the board and teach, encouraging discussion and explanation of strategies, there is an expectation that we will have some textbook work to complete that week. My class knows, however, that once these tasks are completed, they will have some opportunities to apply their learning in a more active and contextualised way. When learning about money, for example, once I have taught about decimals, finding totals, calculating change, and sticking to a budget, I introduce some catalogues and money games to the numeracy table. Then we move on to learning about credit cards and debt; I provide plastic cards (although, by then, a few pupils might have made their own anyway!), calculators, and paper templates for keeping track of money in and out. If computer devices are available, I would also let them have time to explore spreadsheets or similar programmes.

As already mentioned, when you are presenting the class with word problems, change the names to those of some of the learners in your class. By using names that are recognisable to them, word problems become instantly more relevant, meaningful, and easier to imagine.

In the Appendix section, I have included an example of my timetable from recent years (Appendix B) with some idea of the kind of activities I would include in each teaching period. As you can see, I have time for textbook and workbook activities, which follow the curricular programme my school use to ensure progression and moderation throughout the primary years, but I also include opportunities for the learners to put this learning into practice through practical activities, independent applications, and contextual opportunities. It's all about the balance!

As well as these scheduled opportunities, I also timetable a regular slot on a Friday afternoon for reflection on our week's learning, and then learners choose an area to extend in any way they like. This year, the pupils have called it Independent Learning, and it essentially consists of us making a note of what we have learned that week in a big book – what we enjoyed, found challenging, and how we applied it. We then display the book, and everyone chooses something to extend for 30 minutes – the art lesson that they felt didn't go as well as they had hoped, writing their own book with a friend, playing shops, or even fixing corrections from their numeracy textbook (it has happened!). The session has no task boundaries, so pupils can take their learning in any direction they like. It is during these sessions I have seen self-taught stop motion animation discovered, a volume of short stories created, and a small spa business set up. It's my favourite part of the week to observe how my learners apply their learning in different contexts and show their transference of skills.

Another approach to consider is that children love playing teacher. Give them the opportunity to 'be you' in some capacity, and they will enjoy it. I often use this to support peer assessment activities, occasionally asking one child to play teacher, reading out spelling words, or dictation sentences. They then have the other teacher responsibility of marking the work and giving feedback. This role should be rotated so that everyone in the group gets the opportunity to be in charge, but playing schools is a good way to have learners recap or revisit something they have covered previously. And it gives you a great opportunity to observe and listen to discussions around the subject.

Changing Direction

Play is free-flowing, and a context-driven approach requires a lot of flexibility from teachers. If a learner asks a question that is slightly off-topic but nevertheless relevant, answer it. If the class shows an interest when something out of the ordinary happens, dive right into it. If there is a fire drill and it sparks a discussion on the emergency services or "what would we do if . . . ?" (every time!), then take ten minutes or so to just go with it. Encourage curiosity and inquisitiveness.

If you can, create a learning environment where exploration and experimentation are encouraged. I often remind myself of the example of athlete Dick Fosbury.

Traditionally, the jump used by athletes in the high jump was one of a kind of straddle jump. American athlete Dick Fosbury found this technique complicated and instead adopted a more curved run up followed by a backwards 'flop' over the bar. Despite being discouraged by his coach and met with scepticism by critics, Fosbury continued developing his own technique and used it to win gold at the 1968 Olympics and break the world record.

I keep this in mind because, in any learning area, there may be techniques or approaches that we have not considered yet. Imagine being the kind of teacher who encourages students to look for an innovative approach to their learning, uncovering new and effective ways to achieve the desired outcomes. I think this might be a more invigorating way to teach rather than expecting children to learn and apply their skills in the same way.

Your language is also important here; it sets an example for the thoughts and words your learners use. When you are questioning, instead of asking "Can you . . .", ask "How can you . . . ?" It presumes ability and success as well as invites a range of ideas and solutions. Narrate what is happening around you, notice when learners independently access support materials, praise them for using their initiative, and make accessing materials to help up a positive thing. During trickier activities, particularly problem-solving, do a lot of wondering – "I wonder what would happen if you used this instead of that", "I wonder why you picked that material", "I wonder if your idea would help Simon with his problem . . ." If you model inquisitive, enquiring language, exploring ideas, questioning, and recalling, your learners will begin to do that too. Allow opportunities for learners to learn independently – independent learning and/or independent projects.

In my own experience, pupils do not expect to come to school to play. It is not uncommon for pupils to separate their play experiences from their learning experiences and struggle to see the connection between the two. Pupils in the upper years will probably have previous experience of a school where they worked and then they got to play, or play was reserved for certain times of the day or week. The assumption that play is separate from learning is carried throughout the school system. As learners progress through their education, opportunities for play become less and less. Preschool activities include playgroups and playdates; breaks at primary school are known as playtime and take place in the playground. By the time they reach secondary school, playtimes and playgrounds might have become breaks and school grounds.

It is important, therefore, to introduce the change in pedagogy to the class and involve them in the change. Explain that playing can be a method of learning and should not be seen as separate from learning. It might help to change the terminology as explained earlier or focus on the learning that is occurring and the skills being developed. Explain to the class that you are offering contextual learning opportunities (or call it something else that your class is comfortable with – a previous class called it 'plearning' – playing and learning!). If you are new to the play principles in the upper stages or are introducing them with a view to convincing others to join you, how the pupils talk about their new approach is very important. Your colleagues, management team, or parents don't want to hear pupils saying things like, "We just played today". We need to explain to them what we are learning and why we are learning through this approach.

An example of how this might look is:

> "Today we are going to apply our learning on income and expenditure. You will remember that previously you set up your own businesses and have your own bank accounts that I will display on the board, so you know how much money you have. Remember to

make notes in your transaction books of any payments in or out so we can update the bank accounts at the end. You have 20 minutes".

Following the 20 minutes, input the income and expenditure, narrate to the class how this has affected accounts, and discuss how they might make more money or spend less next time. You can ask them how they enjoyed playing businesses, but in general, the focus of the activity is financial education, not playing.

Creating Contextual Learning Opportunities

This is all well and good in theory. Contextual learning opportunities for all learners, continuous provision, incorporating pupil interest and ability, and linking to learning where possible to develop skills and knowledge. Easy, right?!

Obviously not; otherwise, we'd already all be doing it! Introducing the principles of play into an upper-stage classroom is not something I can just tell you how to do. Disappointing, I know! But your class, your teaching style, and your classroom are unique to you. What I can do, however, is tell you some of the methods of bringing these contextual opportunities into the classroom that have worked for me and some of my colleagues.

Something to remember is that, like everything else in our profession, there is no one-size-fits-all approach. As teachers, we need to find what will work for our learners and their specific needs. Whether you have a single stream or a composite class, 18 pupils or 33, with few specific needs or many complex ones, we need to make sure we get it right for every child by tailoring our pedagogy to match our learners.

It is notoriously difficult for teachers to surrender control. It took me quite some time to hand over some control of my classroom to the learners until I accepted that it is not my classroom; it is theirs. We are there to facilitate their learning, but it is their learning environment. You might notice I don't talk about my classroom. It is our classroom.

Simple things like playing music can change the mood of your classroom. It can also help with volume control as quiet music leads to a quiet class – although not all the time! I like study music or sleep music for tasks that require concentration and are more individual, requiring little interaction between peers. The class likes to choose more contemporary music they can sing along to for more relaxed activities, such as practical, creative work. You can even use music as a reward or consequence. A good day or week, and the pupils get to choose the end-of-day music; otherwise, the teacher chooses. My class groans audibly every time I get control of the music choices, and they are subjected to several minutes of 80s electro-pop. However, I have noticed some appreciation for my choices as the year goes on!

The most important thing I have learned from having play in my classroom is to have play around you all the time. Make it predictable and part of your week. It should not be a reward for effort or completing work. If play is offered as an add-on or reward, it is no longer associated with learning. Learning and play are not separate and should not be treated as such. You can make it consistent and predictable by timetabling lessons that learners know will have more playful activities. My class knows that Wednesdays are for Together 31 – playing together for our Health and Wellbeing lesson, linking with our Rights Respecting Schools work- and Tuesday numeracy lessons consist of real-life problem-solving challenges, and Friday afternoons are for independent learning that they can choose. As well as this, I have Play

Trays with resources and games the class has asked for and a Tuff Tray with a weekly challenge. This doesn't change much unless something out of the ordinary happens. Because of this, the class knows that play will be part of their week.

It is also worth noting that some of the elements of play that so many children enjoy – the moving of seats, the music while they work, the time to play games with each other – some other children can find a bit uncomfortable. There are learners who prefer a more regimented, structured approach to their learning. Our job as teachers is to recognise our learners' preferred styles of learning and support them accordingly. If you have pupils who prefer a more traditional approach, during more playful times, offer textbook or worksheet options. During our Together 31 time, I listed a couple of games to choose from for those learners who struggle to make decisions when faced with too many options.

A learning environment that promotes play and play-based learning should encourage learners to independently access opportunities that spark their interest, curiosity, and intrigue. Play for older learners can look more like enquiry, investigation, and exploration, but it all leads to learning experiences. Your classroom should encourage and value play, and the ethos should be one that welcomes questioning and inquisitiveness.

When providing play opportunities, real-life and contextual experiences are vital. Try to provide 'real' resources – an old mobile phone or an unused keyboard rather than plastic toy versions – and use open-ended resources where you can. Loose parts and elements that can be combined will inspire learners rather than guide them. If you leave out a pirate ship, it will be used as a ship. If you leave out a cardboard box, it can be a car, ship, robot head, doll's house, or any number of other inventive creations.

Recording

Allow the learners opportunities to record their learning in their own way as well. As well as the teacher-recorded methods outlined in Chapter 6, I have had learners record their own podcasts and host their own news reports about what they have learned through play. It not only provides you with important evidence but also reaffirms to the children the importance of play in their learning and development. It is such a boost for your play journey as a teacher if your learners can articulate how play is helping them develop their skills and embed the learning that you are teaching them.

A Word of Caution

While coming up with play-based learning for your class, be mindful of concentrating on the fun activities in place of meaningful learning experiences. Pulling out some Play-Doh and instructing your learners to create a depiction of the water cycle while displaying a visual of the cycle on the board might be a lot of fun for your students. There are very few students who don't enjoy spending some time with Play-Doh. But where is the actual learning? The class simply looks at a given visual and follows an instruction to replicate the picture in 3D using a given material. Are they learning about the water cycle, what it is, how it works, and what it means to them in the real world, or are they copying a picture and making it out of Play-Doh?

Ideally, we want to create lessons that hook our learners in, encourage them to ask questions and want to find out more, and provide them with experiences that help them understand better and make meaningful links to the real world.

> **Take Away**
>
> Your playful classroom will have play so embedded into it that learners will know that it is part of their learning and how it supports their understanding. They will not expect it as an add-on that they get it they finish their work or something they do separate from your teaching.
>
> To have a play-based classroom is to have a classroom that encourages and promotes questions, inquisitiveness, and enquiry. Allow learners the opportunity to set themselves challenges, investigate something they are interested in, and be secure that their teacher will support them by indicating where they should look but not telling them what they will find.

References

Vogt, F., Hauser, B., Stebler, R., Rechsteiner, K., and Urech, C. (2018). Learning Through Play – Pedagogy and Learning Outcomes in Early Childhood Mathematics. *European Early Childhood Education Research Journal* 26(4): 589–603. https://doi.org/10.1080/1350293x.2018.1487160

SECTION 3
Practical Lesson Ideas

10 Numeracy and Mathematics

In many instances, play associated with numeracy tends to centre around games that are about the memorising of number facts and mental maths rather than offering opportunities for exploration and reasoning. We often tell learners that there are right and wrong answers to given questions when we could also be giving them a chance to explore other possible solutions or methods of solving a problem.

What follows are some activity ideas that do not always have right and wrong answers, just correct approaches and attitudes towards looking for solutions.

Bingo

Subject:	Numeracy	Area:	Number Processes
Adult Involvement	● ● ● ●		
Resources:	Whiteboards, whiteboard/dry wipe pens You can also use pre-made grids if you have them		
Learning Activity:	This classic game template can be used to reinforce any number of concepts. Start with a 3 x 3 grid. This can simply be drawn on a whiteboard or you can have a template you can use again and again. Ask them to fill their grid with their choice of numbers from the 7 times table (or any multiplication table you have been working on). You then read out calculations, e.g., 7 x 3. Those with 21 on their grids can tick them off, score them out, or mark them however you choose to mark your answers. The first one to score off their numbers wins. In my class, they usually win a sticker!		

(Continued)

70 Practical Lesson Ideas

(Continued)

Subject:	Numeracy	Area:	Number Processes

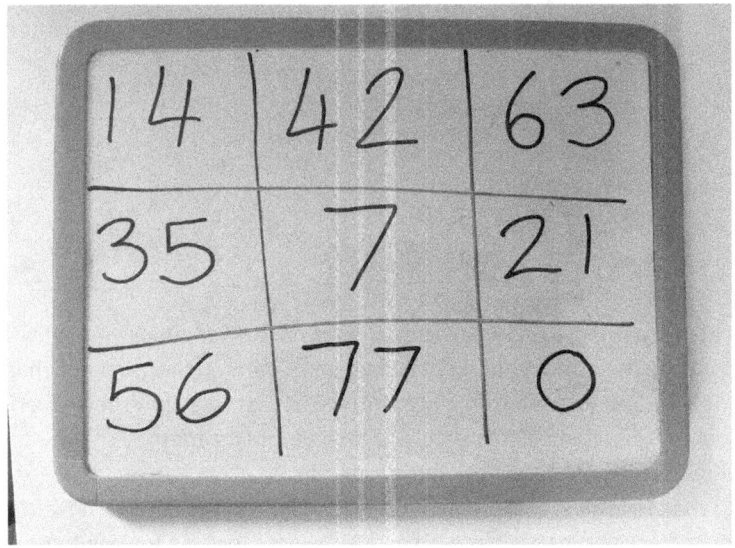

Figure 10.1 Bingo Board

> You can use this template to practice a range of number skills. Instead of multiplication calculations, you can ask them to complete their grids with numbers between 1-14 (or as high as you want), and you read out division calculations, such as 24 ~ 6. Those with 4, tick it off.
> Extend this even further by asking them to choose nine numbers between 1 and 15 (for example) then calling square roots (square root of 81, etc.) or filling in their grid with square numbers between 1 and 144.
> You can also use it to practise halves, doubles, square numbers, cube numbers (or cube roots), or any number pattern that the class has been learning about or need some retrieval practise with.

Jeopardy!

Subject:	Numeracy	Area:	Number Processes

Adult Involvement ● ● ● ●

Resources: Individual whiteboards and whiteboard/dry wipe pens (or paper and pencils) Whiteboard, flipchart, or blackboard to display answers

(Continued)

Subject:	Numeracy	Area:	Number Processes

Learning Activity: As with the TV gameshow, this game is based on you providing an answer and your learners telling you the possible question. In numeracy, this can be met with any number of possible questions all resulting in the same answer.

If you have the time and/or energy, you can set up a board with categories (such as addition, percentages, shape, time, etc.) and levels of difficulty for the learners to select from.

If not, you can simply give the class a number and have them write a question on their board. For example, if I give the number 420, the students might come up with, "What is 210 x 2?" or "What is 418 + 2?"

You can award points for every feasible answer, or you can make it a knockout with any impossible answers leading to that player being 'out'. If you choose to go down this route, I suggest an alternative, independent activity available for these learners as I would never like to have children being 'out' of an activity for very long.

To adapt this game, you could present answers from different areas of maths and numeracy:

Pentagon ("What is a 5-sided shape?" or "What is a shape with five angles?" for example).

50% ("What is 1 as a percentage?" or "What is double 25%?" for example).

3:45 pm ("What is 15mins after 3:30 pm?" or "What is 1545 on the 12-hour clock?" for example).

Tailor your answers to match whatever you are teaching at the time or consolidate previous learning.

A further bonus could be that you also write down a question, and if anyone gets the same one as you, they win ten bonus points, a sticker, or any other prize your class agrees on!

Making Numbers

Subject:	Numeracy	Area:	Number Processes

Adult Involvement

Resources: Playing cards or UNO cards
A grid of numbers 1-30 (not necessary, but helpful)

Learning Activity: Organise the cards so you only have the numbered cards, 1-9.
Arrange your learners as appropriate – working independently or in a small group.
Each team selects four cards at random. They then have a given time to try and make the numbers 1-30 using only the numbers they have.

(Continued)

72 Practical Lesson Ideas

(Continued)

For example:

Figure 10.2 Selected Uno Cards

Numbers selected:		2, 3, 6, 8	
1	3-2	16	8 x 2
2	2	17	8 + 6 + 3
3	3	18	6 x 3
4	6-2	19	(8 x 2) + 3
5	2 + 3	20	(6 x 2) + 8

You can adapt this activity for challenge or support by selecting specific cards for a team, giving them fewer numbers to find (e.g., 1-20), allowing them to use the same number more than once, giving them five cards, and/or allowing them to use calculators.

Darts Dice

Subject:	Numeracy	Area:	Number Processes
Adult Involvement		● ●	
Resources:	Dice - three per group of learners (or one dice they roll three times) Paper and pencils (or individual whiteboards and dry wipe pens)		

(Continued)

Subject:	Numeracy	Area:	Number Processes

Learning Activity: Split the learners into pairs or small groups.
Each player has a starting score of 101.
The first player rolls the dice and subtracts the three numbers from their total. The next player repeats, and the first player to reach zero wins.

Figure 10.3 Darts Dice

You can discuss with the learners if it is easier for them to subtract the three numbers individually or add them first and then subtract the total. Or any other strategy they may have.

If you group the learners by ability, you can add challenges by starting with a higher score, e.g., 301. Learners roll two dice and multiply the two numbers to get the total they must subtract. Alternatively, you can have them roll three dice and multiply the numbers for the total they have to take away each time, or double (or treble!) the numbers shown on the dice before calculating the total they need to subtract.

Support can be added with a smaller starting score and providing number lines or a 100-square.

Target Slide

Subject:	Numeracy	Area:	Number Processes

Adult Involvement

Resources: Targets – these can be printed targets or drawn on the desk with chalk pen as shown further on
Counters or similar

(Continued)

74 Practical Lesson Ideas

(Continued)

Subject:	Numeracy	Area:	Number Processes
Learning Activity:	Depending on your focus, this can be used as an addition or subtraction activity. Addition: Players have three counters each. Using the targets, learners take it in turns sliding their counters towards the target. They then add up their scores to calculate their total score. The winner is the player with the highest score. Subtraction: You can adapt this to be more like a game of darts. Each player starts with 100 and subtracts their score.		
	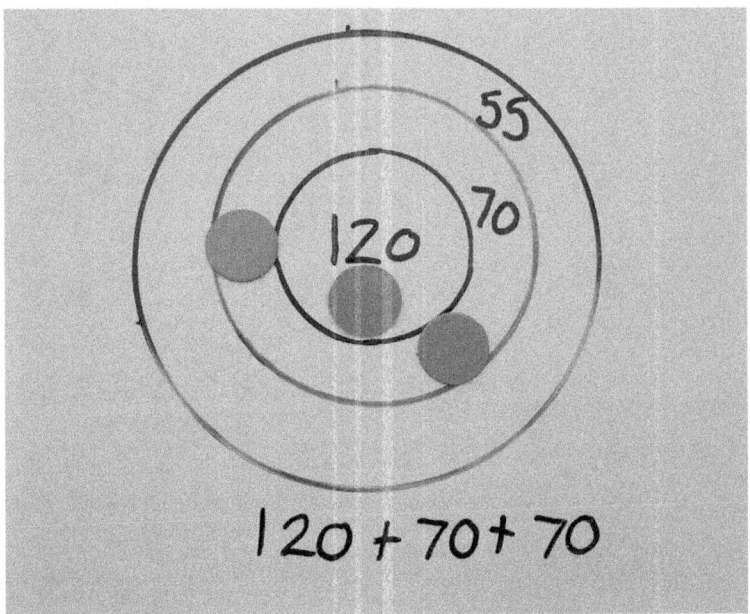 Figure 10.4 Target Slide		
	To support learners, you can change the number of counters they have, throwing one at a time or providing them with additional aids such as 100-squares or number lines. You can also change the numbers on the target for easier addition or subtraction. To challenge, have a target with more complex numbers or counters that represent different values – (green counter x2, red counter x3) and have them multiply their scores before adding them. You can then link to the BODMAS (PEDMAS) rule.		

Greater Than, Less Than

Subject:	Numeracy	Area:	Number – Place Value
Adult Involvement		● ●	
Resources:	Whiteboards, whiteboard/dry wipe pens Alternatively, you can write on desks using dry wipe pens or chalk pens Dice – place value dice are ideal, but regular six-sided dice will work just as well		

(Continued)

Subject:	Numeracy	Area:	Number – Place Value
Learning Activity:	Working in pairs, Learner 1 rolls the dice. If you have place value dice, this will create a three-digit number, e.g., 600 and 40 and 2 = 642. If you have regular dice, roll it three times to create a 3-digit number, e.g., 5 and 1 and 3 = 513. Write this 3-digit number down. Learner 2 repeats, rolling the dice and writing down their number. The pair must then agree on whether the first number is greater than or less than the first number and draw the appropriate symbol between them, e.g., 642 > 513.		

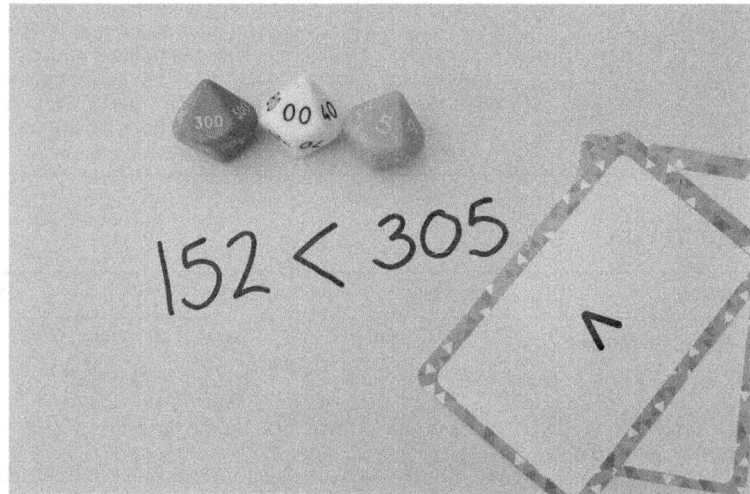

Figure 10.5 Greater Than or Less Than

You can adapt this activity to include a competitive element – whichever player rolls the biggest number wins a point. Or whoever draws the correct symbol first. Or have > and < cards that they can play; whoever lays their card first wins.

You can support learners by starting off with single-digit or two-digit numbers and challenging them with four- or five-digit numbers. You can also add the criteria that both players start with 2,000 and must roll their dice to find the other three digits.

Around the World

Subject:	Numeracy	Area:	Number Processes
Adult Involvement		● ●	
Resources:	None		

(Continued)

Practical Lesson Ideas

(Continued)

Subject:	Numeracy	Area:	Number Processes
Learning Activity:	This requires quick-fire questions, so you might want to have some prepared on flashcards if you can, though you can also just come up with them on the spot.		
	Player 1 stands behind the person next to them. You fire a question at them both (or show them a flashcard). The first one to answer correctly wins the round. If it is the student already standing, they move on to stand behind the next player. If it is the player sitting, player 1 takes their seat, and they move on to the next player. Continue until every learner has had a chance to play. The person who is left standing at the end of the game starts the game the next time.		
	If you have a large class, you might want to do this with groups - you can nominate a child to facilitate the game if you give them flashcards with answers or a calculator to check the correct answers!		
	You can tailor the game to focus on a particular area if there is something you are working on - all the questions can be about a specific multiplication table, division facts, or properties of shapes, etc.		

Beach Fun

Subject:	Numeracy	Area:	Number Processes
Adult Involvement		● ●	
Resources:	A beach ball (or two if you have a large class)		
Learning Activity:	Write some calculations on a beach ball - one calculation on each section should be enough, but you can add more if you want. Tailor the questions to your class or separate the class into groups with a beach ball for each group and differentiate the questions on the ball.		
	Read out a calculation from the ball and throw it to a student, who must attempt to answer it as they catch it. If they answer correctly, they can choose a question and throw the ball to another learner. Repeat until everyone has had a turn of answering a question.		
	You can theme the questions such as facts from the eight times table or subtraction from 100. You can add to the game by giving points for correct answers or giving the class the challenge of getting the ball around the class within a limited time. Or have a personal best time recorded somewhere and try to beat it.		

Back to Back

Subject:	Maths	Area:	Number Processes
Adult Involvement		● ●	
Resources:	Individual Whiteboards and dry wipe pens (or similar)		

(Continued)

Subject:	Maths	Area:	Number Processes

Learning Activity: Group learners into groups of 3 with a similar ability level.
Two players sit or stand back-to-back, and when the third player says 'go', they write a number on their boards.
The third player tells them the sum of the two numbers. The first player to work out what their opponent's number is wins a point.
Rotate so the third player plays the winner.
You can give boundaries to the game to support learners – the numbers must be below 50 or 100.
You can adapt the game by having the third player calculate the product of the two numbers, rather than the sum, and giving limits to the numbers, such as below 10 or 20.

Noughts and Crosses (Tic-Tac-Toe)

Subject:	Maths	Area:	Number Processes

Adult Involvement ● ●

Resources: Chalk Pens (or individual whiteboards and dry wipe pens or paper and pencils)
Flashcards (can be tailored to focus on a specific theme, e.g., the 7 times table)

Learning Activity: As in the original noughts and crosses, learners play in pairs. They start by drawing out a 3 x 3 grid (on the table with chalk pens or on their board or paper). They can play rock, paper, scissors to decide who goes first.
The first player picks the first flashcard. If they can answer the question correctly, they can place their mark. Then it is player 2's turn. If either player gets their question wrong, they miss their turn.
The winner is the first player to get a line of three in a row, vertically, horizontally, or diagonally.

Binary Coding

Subject:	Maths	Area:	Computer Science/ Number Patterns

Adult Involvement ● ●

Resources: Jotters, paper, or whiteboards to write on.

Learning Activity: Explain the Binary Coding system to your class.
Demonstrate using the binary columns showing powers of 2 and how the digits 0 and 1 can be used to represent the numbers 0-5. Then, challenge your class to represent further numbers. You can differentiate with the quantity of numbers you ask them to represent.
Once the learners have the hang of the coding system, you can ask them to devise a use for this code – it could be to have a secret passcode to the classroom or to create a number-to-letter code that can then be used to create messages or give directions.

78 Practical Lesson Ideas

Number Relay

Subject:	Maths, Numeracy	Area:	Number Processes

Adult Involvement ● ● ● ●

Resources: A page of calculations – set at a level appropriate for your learners (one page for each team)
You could do this on a digital device to save paper

Learning Activity: Group learners into small teams – matched by ability.
Teams must complete the calculations on the sheet, but they can only complete one at a time and then tag their teammate in to solve the next one. The winning team is the first to complete all the calculations correctly.
Depending on your space (or how you prefer to manage your class), you can have each team sit around a table and pass the sheet around, or you can have them run to the sheet and back to high-five their teammate and complete the race like a relay.
If you are focussing on a specific times table, for example, you can give the same questions over a few lessons to increase speed and fluency with the facts. Simple plastic wallets can be useful as you can put the sheets into them, have the students write with dry-wipe pens and simply wipe the answers off to be used again next time.

Plan a Journey

Subject:	Maths	Area:	Time

Adult Involvement ● ●

Resources: Timetables (bus, train, etc.)

Learning Activity: Using the timetables, ask your learners to plan a journey from point A to destination B.
Depending on the level of challenge required, give them constraints such as having to leave after X time or arriving before Y time (or both!).
You can add stop-off points on the way or ask them to plan a journey for which you know there is no direct transport link. Planning a change of train, or even better, changing from a train to a bus and therefore considering the time required to travel from the train station to the bus station, will level up this activity to its required challenge level.
This can also be used to support the transition to high school if learners will be required to catch a bus to their new school. Plan their journeys†with a real-life context that will be useful to them – look at the bus routes that pass near the school and stops near their homes to†plan which bus they will need to take and what time they might need to leave in the morning. You can also look at the route for coming†home as well.

Calculating Speeds

Subject:	Numeracy/Maths	Area:	Speed, Distance, Time

Adult Involvement

Resources: Marbles, stopwatches, junk

Learning Activity: This series of lessons links very closely with the STEM activities mentioned previously. It uses STEM to put a numeracy concept into a context that is designed to deepen understanding and application for learners. You could teach it over a series of Numeracy or Maths lessons or as a whole day dedicated to the application of this concept after you have taught it.

Stage 1 - Teach the class about the formula for calculating speed, distance, and time. Provide examples and perhaps set them some theoretical questions to complete; I use our textbooks.

Stage 2 - Using stopwatches, the learners time themselves, carrying out some activities, such as 50-star jumps or writing their names. They then use the speed, distance, and time formula to calculate their speed. If I completed 50 star jumps in one minute, I did them at a speed of 300 star jumps per hour. If it took me five seconds to write my name, I wrote it in 12 names per minute.

Stage 3 - Learners create a simple, straight marble ramp using a limited selection of materials and a given timescale. (This introduces different skills in addition to numeracy while supporting the play element - timekeeping, resourcefulness, and initiative. Interdisciplinary learning can deepen understanding of concepts). Learners are then challenged with timing their marble's journey down the construction. You can keep a record of these speeds.

Stage 4 - Using the ramps previously created, or creating a new ramp, learners are challenged to calculate the speed of their marble. If required, you can support them in recalling the information they will need to do this - time and distance. They practised timing the marble previously, so now they need to work out the distance travelled.

If you want to or have the time to, you can level this up further by setting a class challenge of trying to create the slowest marble ramp. The marble must complete the circuit but with the biggest recorded time. The class, by this point, may have worked out that this would require either a very long ramp or a very slow marble. How they set about creating this can be wonderful to watch. I had one child create a kind of drain swirl to slow the marble on its way down!

Discounts

Subject:	Numeracy	Area:	Percentages

Adult Involvement

Resources: Shopping catalogues (physical or online), play money, card
Travel brochures

(Continued)

Subject:	Numeracy	Area:	Percentages
Learning Activity:	Following some work on calculating percentages of a number, work with the class on how we calculate percentage discounts, such as calculating 20% off. This can link to calculating the VAT on certain items, but you could also set up some real-life activities to play with.		
	Setting up a shop with priced items, give pupils a discount card. You can differentiate the amounts to meet the needs of the learner - 50% off for those who need some support or 20% for those who can handle the challenge. You can also tailor the prices of your items to match your learners.		
	With a shopkeeper armed with either a calculator or cheat sheet with answers, pupils must work out how much they need to pay once they have taken off their discount. The shopkeeper will peer assess to ensure they are calculating correctly. Don't forget to rotate your shopkeepers.		
	A similar activity can be done with bigger numbers, by asking the pupils to book travel and accommodation holidays or create holiday packages.		

Angles in Action

Subject:	Maths	Area:	Angles
Adult Involvement	●●		
Resources:	Junk, toy cars, tape measure or rulers Protractors, sturdy card, split pins		
Learning Activity:	Start by creating an angle arm to help measure the size of your angles.		
	Challenge your learners to create a ramp for the cars. Give them a specific target, such as creating a ramp that will allow their car to travel the furthest distance. Have them measure the angle of their ramp and the distance travelled. Try some different angles and try to find the optimal ramp for maximum distance.		
	If you have previously done some work on speed, distance, and time, you can use this to compare angles and levels of steepness with speed.		

Simon Says

Subject:	Maths	Area:	Angles
Adult Involvement	●●●		
Resources:	None		
Learning Activity:	This short activity can be used as a simple recap or warm-up before a lesson on angles.		
	Have your learners stand up and, on your command, make an angle with their arms - "Simon Says, acute angle", "Simon Says, an angle greater than 90+".		
	You can adapt the game to suit the needs of your class - if you don't say "Simon Says" and the pupils make the angle, they can be out, or you can just score the teacher a point in a teacher vs class game.		

Follow the Directions

Subject:	Maths	Area:	Angles - turning and bearings Co-ordinates

Adult Involvement ● ●

Resources: Grids of some sort - you can mark a giant one out on the floor with masking tape or create smaller ones on A4 paper. If you slip them inside a plastic folder or wallet, you can reuse them
If you are using smaller grids, character figures are useful - wooden dolls, Lego characters, or similar

Learning Activity: Learners are required to create a sequence of movements using directions and angles to describe turns.
Remind them 90⁕ = a quarter turn, so you will need to give direction - clockwise or anticlockwise. You can use diagonal movements in your grid as well with 45⁕ turns.
Once they have completed their sequence of movements, ask someone else to follow them. You can film the sequence for them to check if they are correct or have a specific grid point that they should finish on if they have followed the directions accurately.
You can adapt this by having grid references and adding in learning about co-ordinates or using it with a coding programme on a digital device to link in some digital technologies or digital science.
You could also use it with a treasure hunt theme, as 'pirates' who need to follow the directions to uncover where the buried treasure can be found.

Show Your Learning - Classifying Angles

Subject:	Maths	Area:	Angles

Adult Involvement ●

Resources: Range of materials - Card/Paper, iPads or Netbooks, Straws, Pegboards and elastic bands, K*Nex, Lego . . .

Learning Activity: This type of activity can be done following pretty much any learning, but I am using the classification of angles to illustrate how it might be delivered.
Recap previous learning with the class, writing up on the board the main classification categories of angles - acute, right, obtuse, straight, and reflex, with example measurements next to them, for example.
Ask the class how engaging your board is - not very! Challenge them to share their learning in a more engaging way that can be used to help others. Allow them to choose resources from a table of materials and give them a time limit to complete the task.
If they are stuck for ideas, perhaps they could create a video demonstrating the different types of angles, a PowerPoint or Google Slides presentation, a song or rap about the categories or simply their own, more engaging poster.

82 Practical Lesson Ideas

Deal or No Deal

Subject:	Numeracy/Maths	Area:	Certainty, Risk, and Chance

Adult Involvement

● ●

Resources: Cards with money amounts (or individual whiteboards and dry wipe pens)
Learning Activity: Just as in the TV game show, have money amounts written on cards or whiteboards and randomly give them out to the class. For extra secrecy, you could put the amounts in sealed envelopes, but this is not very eco-friendly or sustainable. However you do it, make sure the learners can't see the amount on their card.
One player comes to the front of the class and hands you their card (so absolutely no chance of peeking!).
They select classmates to turn over their amounts, and every three turns or so, you can offer them a trade-in amount for their card.
You can keep a display of which amounts have been accounted for and, as a result, what the chances are of their card being valuable.
You can also develop an alternative version of this game that involves real rewards or consequences for the learner (or class) - extra homework, arts and crafts time, outside play, 20-lines, etc.), and the game becomes a bit more risky!

Estimating a Metre

Subject:	Maths	Area:	Measuring

Adult Involvement

Resources: A metre stick (or tape measure)
Learning Activity: Group learners into small teams.
Challenge the teams to find 2-4 (or a range of your choice) items around the classroom that, when put together, will measure approximately 1 metre.
Give them a time limit to add a challenge. You can also award the team with the closest estimate points or a prize of some kind (I always have stickers around for this type of activity!).

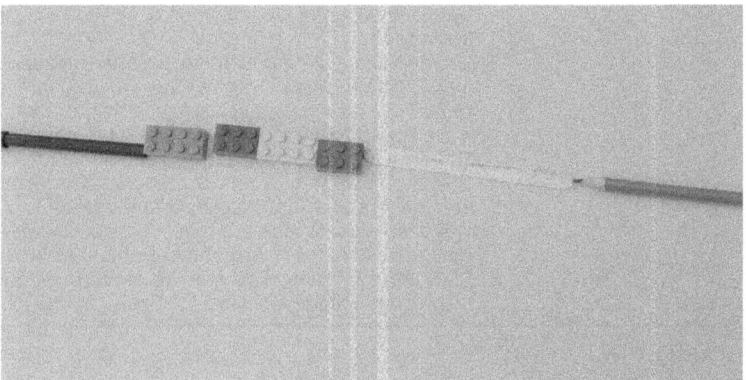

Figure 10.6 Estimating Length

You can adapt this short activity to find items that will result in a more specific measurement (e.g., 86cm) and/or have the class convert their measurements from metres into centimetres or millimetres.

11 Literacy

There are opportunities to develop literacy in most aspects of play. Having lists and reading materials in role-play opportunities, leaving clipboards, paper, and pens in the construction area, or having letters scattered around your Tuff Tray. Not to mention the conversations you will overhear and the vocabulary used during these times. But there are some Literacy-specific tasks for you to consider as well.

Listening and Talking

Give your class the opportunity to listen to an audiobook. It's simple but effective. I have used audiobooks in my class for years. After having the whole class listen to a book or an extract from one, I try to provide it as an option during reading time. There are some children for whom reading for pleasure will always be elusive. They just don't enjoy it. Perhaps they have barriers to reading, and the actual reading is too difficult for them to find any pleasure in, or perhaps they just haven't found a text they find joy in. No matter the reason, I always think that this doesn't have to mean they can't enjoy stories or books in another way, particularly if you can create a way for more than one learner to listen to the same story at the same time, either in a quiet space or with multiple headphones connected.

A lot of games played in the early years can be adapted to use throughout the school at any stage. While these games involve listening and talking, the vocabulary and language skills developed will hopefully transfer into reading and writing activities as well. Anyone who has been involved in talking for writing will know how inextricably they are linked.

I Spy

In the early years, you might play a game of I Spy something coloured blue, or I Spy something beginning with T. Why not change this to I Spy something translucent, or I Spy a tree as tall as a _____ and use the game as a warm-up activity to develop vocabulary or descriptive language.

The Minister's Cat

Subject:	Literacy	Area:	Vocabulary

Adult Involvement

Resources: None
Learning Activity: With a steady rhythm, the class chant, "The Minister's Cat is a . . ." and one by one, pupils fill in the blank – you can set the task to be adventurous adjectives, adjectives starting with vowels, adjectives progressing through the alphabet . . . your imagination can be as creative as you like!
The Minister's Cat is an angry cat.
The Minister's Cat is a bashful cat.
The Minister's Cat is a cantankerous cat.
The Minister's Cat is an opportunistic cat.
The Minister's Cat is a despondent cat.

The Shopping Game

This game relies on memory but can be used to develop language as well.

Subject:	Literacy	Area:	Vocabulary/Listening and Talking

Adult Involvement

Resources: None
Learning Activity: This game relies on memory but can be used to develop language as well.
The first player completes the sentence, "I went shopping, and I bought a . . ."
The second player has to repeat player 1's shopping list and add one of their own, and so on.
You can add support to the game by going through the alphabet or only adding items with a given characteristic (e.g., beginning with C or things you can see in the classroom).
I went shopping, and I bought an <u>apple</u>.
I went shopping, and I bought an apple and a <u>ball</u>.
I went shopping, and I bought an apple, a ball, and a <u>curtain</u>.

Getting to Know You

This is very similar to the Shopping Game, but the context is more about the learners and allows them opportunities to get to know each other.

Subject:	Literacy	Area:	Vocabulary/Listening & Talking

Adult Involvement

Resources: None

(Continued)

Subject:	Literacy	Area:	Vocabulary/Listening & Talking

Learning Activity:	Organise your class so they are sitting around tables in groups of about four or five (or on the floor in a circle). Decide who will start, and this person introduces themselves and says something they enjoy. The next person must repeat the first person's information before providing theirs. The third person must repeat the information from the first two before their turn, and so on. My name is Peter, and I like football. Peter likes football. I am Rebecca, and I like chocolate. Peter likes football, Rebecca likes chocolate. My name is Sam, and I like going to the beach . . . At any time, you can ask someone in the group to tell you something about the others in their group. You can adapt the game to have a certain theme (films we love, places we've been, pets, favourite colours . . .)

Independent Talks or Presentations

This is very similar to the Shopping Game, but the context is more about the learners and allows them opportunities to get to know each other.

Subject:	Literacy	Area:	Vocabulary/Listening & Talking

Adult Involvement

Resources:	None
Learning Activity:	Challenge your class with a mission to create a short talk on a subject of their choice. You can give them a general topic if you want to keep it related to curricular plans - Favourite songs/singers, TV shows, sport. Give the learners some time and support, if they need it, to prepare their talk. You can encourage them to write it down first, but perhaps they would prefer to draw symbols to help them remember what to say. You can differentiate this by changing the allotted time for their talk - 1 minute is quite long when you think about it! You can also allow them to create visual aids to support them or allow them to work with peers.

Writing

A simple way to make writing playful is to put no boundaries on it whatsoever. Of course, by asking your learners to write at all, the activity is no longer truly play, but if writing is the only thing you are asking them to do, play can come into the activity in so many other ways.

During Free Write Fridays, I have often had a range of materials available for writing, and I set a timer for the activity to take place, usually about 30 minutes. That is it. The students can choose to write in their jotters, on lined paper, on blank paper, or on the desk with chalk pens. They can choose to write on their own or collaboratively with peers. They can type it. They can write an imaginative piece about new dimension portals or a factual piece about what their plans are for the weekend. They can write a comic strip, a story, a news report, a diary entry, or a rant about how much they disliked my numeracy lesson earlier that day. I do ask that they don't write anything hurtful about another person or anything inappropriate for their age and stage - but all of this is part of our classroom ethos anyway and not specific to our free writing sessions.

Writing can be tricky for many children, but it is a necessary part of learning and teaching. Opportunities like this remove as much of the stress and pressure as you possibly can. It puts writing in a playful context, a fun space where those who struggle with it may actually find a way to enjoy it in these moments.

Nonsense Sentences

Subject:	Literacy	Area:	Writing - Sentence Structure
Adult Involvement		● ● ●	
Resources:	Paper and pencils		
Learning Activity:	After teaching your class about nouns, verbs, conjunctions (or connectives), and so on, you can use these parts of language to play around with sentence structure. Demonstrate how a simple sentence has meaning with a noun (subject) and a verb - The cat purred. A girl ran. A clock ticks. You can then have them write a noun (subject) or two on pieces of paper and leave them in a pile in the middle of the table. Then, have them write some verbs on more pieces of paper and create another pile. It might be useful to agree on a tense. Then, have each learner pick a noun and a verb to create their simple sentence. The cat ticks. A girl purred. You can build on this by adding prepositions, further nouns (objects), time sequencers (next, later, finally), and then try to combine the nonsense sentences from the table into a nonsense paragraph.		

10-Word Stories

Subject:	Literacy	Area:	Writing - Vocabulary
Adult Involvement		●	
Resources:	Paper and pencils (or whiteboards and pens; desks and chalk pens . . .)		
Learning Activity:	Challenge your learners to write a simple but complete story using only ten words - no more, no less. This can help learners consider the words they use and replace them with more concise vocabulary. "Ran very fast" can become "sprinted"; "looked around all over the place" can become "explored extensively". They can work alone or with a partner. Give them a time limit and ask them to read their stories out at the end. Have the class check the word count. The cat woke up, caught a mouse, and fell asleep. A lion escaped captivity, ran for an hour before recapture. You can adapt this by providing a story start or changing the number of words allowed.		

Literacy 87

Alphabet Stories

Subject:	Literacy	Area:	Writing - Vocabulary

Adult Involvement

Resources: Paper and pencils (or whiteboards and pens; Desks and chalk pens . . .)
Learning Activity: Challenge your learners to write a simple but complete sentence where each word starts with the letter after the previous one. You can have everyone start with 'A' and model some examples until they get the hang of it. It doesn't have to be a precise and factually correct sentence, but it does need to make grammatical sense.
Adam brought Catherine dinner every Friday.
After bedtime, cats don't ever fight.
Once everyone has the hang of it, you can have them start with any word they like before handing their paper to their partner or around their table to try and complete an alphabet sentence.
You can support learners by providing a sentence start for them to complete - Adam bought Catherine _____ every _____.
You can challenge learners by asking them to provide an adjective and/or an adverb in their sentence. Or each word has to start with the last letter of the word before.
Tricky, yes. See, everything gets stranger right then!

Consequences

Subject:	Literacy	Area:	Writing - Sentence Structure

Adult Involvement

Resources: Paper and pencils or Whiteboards and dry-wipe pens
Learning Activity: Many of us have played the game of Consequences - it may be called a different name in different parts of the world.
You ask everyone to write a name at the top of a sheet of paper, then fold it. The paper is then passed to the next person, who writes another name, folds the paper again, and passes it on. The next people write a location, what they said, and a consequence. Inevitably, the finished sheet makes no sense and reads something like this:
Taylor Swift
(and) Winnie the Pooh
(met at) The Cinema
(they said) Sausages taste great on a sandwich
(and the consequence was . . .) There was a solar eclipse.
This game is silly and fun, but it can also be used to teach some useful literacy tools.
Ask learners to write a noun (subject), a preposition, a location, an adjective, another noun (object), a verb, an adverb, and a consequence, and your silly sentence is uplevelled to:
A cat (was) beside Edinburgh Castle (with a) gigantic table (that was) jumping slowly. The consequence was that the chicken crossed the road.
It's still silly and fun, but now it's teaching your class about other features of language, too.

88 *Practical Lesson Ideas*

Openers

Subject:	Literacy	Area:	Writing - Sentence Structure

Adult Involvement

Resources: Dry-wipe cube (or one you can insert words or activities into each side)

Learning Activity: Using a dry wipe cube (or similar), challenge your learners to start their sentences with different openers.

On your wipe-clean cube, write Noun, Adjective, Verb, Adverb, Preposition, and Conjunction/Connective. Learners roll the dice and must write a sentence starting with the resulting part of speech. You can even give the class a sentence to manipulate to start accordingly.

For example: The cat was sitting on the rug and licked its paw.
Noun – The cat sat on the mat and licked its paw.
Adjective – Furry paws were being licked by the cat sitting on the rug.
Verb – Sitting on the rug, the cat licked its paw.
Adverb – Calmly sitting on the rug, the cat licked its paw.
Preposition – On the rug, the cat licked its paws.
Conjunction – While sitting on the rug, the cat licked its paws.

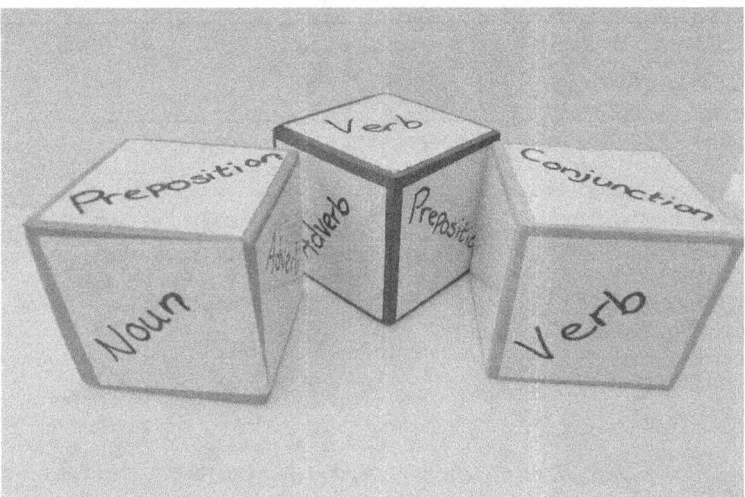

Figure 11.1 Openers Cubes

You can support learners by reducing the choices on the dice and repeating the same two or three multiple times.

Blankety-Blank

Subject:	Literacy	Area:	Reading - Inferring Writing - Vocabulary

Adult Involvement

Literacy 89

(Continued)

Subject:	Literacy	Area:	Reading – Inferring Writing – Vocabulary
Resources:	Whiteboard to display paragraph Jotters or individual whiteboards		
Learning Activity:	Prepare a passage with words missing (blanks). Number the blanks. It is helpful if the passage is from a book that they are familiar with or about a subject that is known to them. Have the learners write the numbers in their jotter and come up with a word that could fit each blank. Read the passage aloud to them a couple of times to help them come up with appropriate words. Once completed, you can score the answers – 1 for an acceptable answer; 2 for the exact same answer from the original passage. You can award prizes or rewards for those scoring over a certain threshold or simply for the highest score in the class. My class particularly enjoyed having the Blankety Blank theme tune played before and after each lesson to give it a lovely game show feeling!		

Connect 4 or 4-in-a-Row

Subject:	Literacy	Area:	Vocabulary
Adult Involvement		● ●	
Resources:	A Connect 4 (4-in-a-Row) game Or pre-printed grid of about 8 x 8 spaces (if you place it inside a plastic wallet or laminate, then you can use this resource many times) Word Cards – e.g., happy, sad, nice, good, bad		
Learning Activity:	Either individually or in teams of two, players play gainst another player or team. Allocate each side a symbol (e.g., X and O) or a colour. Player/Team 1 picks a card and needs to come up with a synonym for that word. If they can, they play their counter or colour/mark a space on the grid. Repeat for the other side. The team that can get a row of four colours/counters wins. You can add a timer of five seconds (or whatever suits your learners) to place some pressure on coming up with new words. Alternatively, you can ask learners to come up with antonyms rather than synonyms or alternative words for 'said' or 'went', depending on what your class focus is.		

Dominoes or Loop Cards

Subject:	Literacy	Area:	Writing – Sentence Structure
Adult Involvement		● ●	
Resources:	Dry-wipe cube (or one you can insert words or activities into each side)		

(Continued)

90 Practical Lesson Ideas

(Continued)

Subject:	Literacy	Area:	Writing – Sentence Structure
Learning Activity:	Dominoes or Loop Cards can be designed to fit any context with a matching element. This example can be for synonyms, matching words with another that has a similar meaning. Linking individual words with their contractions.		

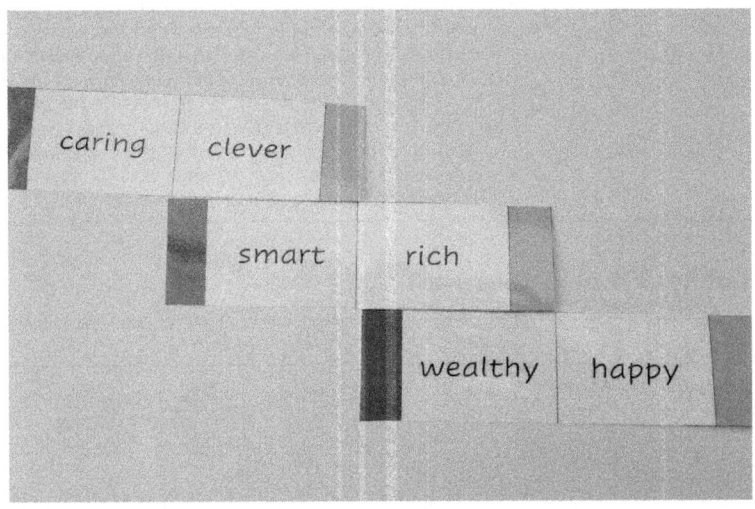

Figure 11.2 Synonym Cards

You could also use this resource to play with antonyms or contractions, matching two words with their contractions:
she had = she'd
will not = won't

Writing Provocations

Subject:	Literacy	Area:	Writing for a purpose
Adult Involvement		● ●	
Resources:	Paper and pencils Or a digital device for typing		

(Continued)

Subject:	Literacy	Area:	Writing for a purpose
Learning Activity:	Learners can find extra intrinsic motivation to succeed in their writing if they see a purpose to it. The best writing I have had from my class comes when they see a reason for it. Here are some purposeful writing ideas that you can build towards with your lessons on the tools for writing that are required. Persuasive Writing: - Write to you (or the headteacher) to persuade you or them that the class should have something. Perhaps a class party at the end of term or an extra break outside? - Set up a scenario like the book "The Day the Crayons Quit". I have seen colleagues have the chairs go on strike or the pencils quit - and the class has to persuade the items to come back to work. - Write to a local business or members of the community, asking them to donate to an event or to support a local fundraiser. There may be a local charity shop in need of some support or a national fundraising event your class could be part of. Imaginative Writing: - Write and publish a class book. You can self-publish your book for free. A quick internet search will find you several sites that will allow you to do this. Alternatively, you can create an electronic version and share it with parents via whichever platform(s) you use to communicate with home. - You could create a picture book for younger children. You can ask each learner to create one or allow them to work in groups. It can help explain the different roles of authors and illustrators if you allow them to share the responsibilities. They can then bring their books to a younger class and read to them. - Create your own comic books or eBooks using any number of apps or programmes. Many school devices will come with a writing app that is already built in. - Allow your learners to read each other's work and write reviews. Encourage them to give each other feedback and how to write reviews in an honest but kind way. Report Writing: - Find out if another class is learning about something similar and could maybe use your class reports to help with their learning - even for a reading comprehension task, and your learners could set the questions. - Display the reports in an area where others can see them. Or invite visitors in to read the reports. Better still, if you have a local expert or group that you could share the reports with, e.g., if the class has written reports on the effects of pollution, is there a local conservation group or council who would be interested in reading them?		

Editors

Subject:	Literacy	Area:	Writing
Adult Involvement		● ●	
Resources:	Prepared passages for learners to mark or edit Highlighters or 'teacher' pens		

(Continued)

92 Practical Lesson Ideas

(Continued)

Subject:	Literacy	Area:	Writing
Learning Activity:	Have your learners become teachers. Give them a passage that they need to mark and edit. You can tailor the passage in a way that focusses on any element you need. Capital Letters – give them a passage with lots of names and/or countries without capital letters that they need to identify and add in. Commas – a passage full of lists needs commas to edit it correctly. Speech Marks – a conversation would help with speech marks. I also like to use 'said' for every piece of speech and ask the class to replace some of these with more adventurous words. You can develop this with more challenge for students who need it by creating longer passages, misspelling using homophones or commonly mis-spelt words, or using vocabulary they are unfamiliar with. Once the skills have been developed, you can use this teacher role play to help with peer assessments.		

Spelling Activities

Spelling is something that can be quite a frustrating skill to embed. There are many occasions where I have supported learners who progress well through spelling schemes, who complete workbooks and spelling tests to a good standard, but who can struggle to transfer this into their independent writing.

These activities can help transfer the spelling of individual words into working and long-term memory.

Spelling Teacher

There are usually several spelling groups in a class, and managing them all can be quite the juggle. If you can train a selected group (or two if you are lucky!) to manage themselves, then your workload becomes a lot more manageable. My class does spelling four times a week, culminating in a weekly spelling test. One group is given a list of words produced by me and given the challenge to learn them all before the test at the end of the week. I worked with them to develop how they wanted to do this, and they decided that each week a different member of the group would be the 'teacher' and come up with lessons to teach the spellings.

I have seen them being asked to write the words out multiple times, speed spelling races, a quiz-style buzzer competition, and a Spelling Bee format. At the end of the week, the group sits their test, and their 'teacher' that week marks it. Usually, with a lovely little comment at the bottom. I only need to look at the tests to see that this is working for them.

Spelling Stations

Subject:	Literacy	Area:	Writing – Spelling
Adult Involvement		● ● ●	
Resources:	Depending on your stations: Play-Doh, salt or sand, computers/netbooks/iPads, chalk pens or dry wipe pens, paint, paintbrushes, paper		

Literacy 93

(Continued)

Subject:	Literacy	Area:	Writing – Spelling

Learning Activity: Play-Doh – use the play doh to manipulate and make the words on your list.
Salt/Sand – write the words using your finger to trace the words out.
Typing – type your words on something like Word. Play around with the font to make your words stand out.
Alternative surfaces – rather than simply writing your words on paper, use dry wipe pens to write on the window or chalk pens to write on the tables.

Figure 11.3 Spelling Activities

Painting – paint your words. If you don't want to deal with the potential mess of actual paint, painting on paper with water also works. Or, in the nicer weather, get outside and paint with water on the playground!
Reminders – ask your learners to come up with ways to remember any tricky aspects of their words. I regularly use the phrase "Oh, you lucky duck" to remind learners of the spelling OULD for could, should, and would. It's silly, but it reminds them!

Reading

I find that reading and writing are so closely linked that it is difficult to provide you with ideas for play in writing that don't involve some element of reading. As such, many of the writing activities suggested above will inevitably support your learners' reading in some way as well.

Nevertheless, reading can be a playful activity if you create opportunities for choice. In my library corner, I try to have as much variety as I can, with novels, picture books, comics, magazines, and age-appropriate newspapers. I have a mixture of fact and fiction, and I have yet to meet a class that is not fascinated by the Guinness Book of Records, so there is always at least one copy of that available!

You can also create a play-based reading activity by including text in another curricular activity, asking your learners to follow a vague set of instructions (use these materials to create a card for someone you care about), or encourage them to read the instructions for an unfamiliar board game independently.

Reading is playful if it is something a child chooses to do and something they have chosen to read. As soon as you start asking them to answer questions about something they have read or write a review about their reading material, you take away some of the play element. You do, however, add to the learning element, and, as mentioned before, it is all about balance.

Book Club

Allow your learners some time to read for enjoyment with each other. Allow them to create their own book club with classmates who are interested in the same kind of books. They can set their own homework or how many pages they should read. You can ask them to read aloud to each other in their group. You can also give them some challenges to do within their group – create a new front cover for their book, discuss what they think will happen next, who is their favourite character, or if they had to add a new character, who would it be? Once they have finished their book, they can write a short review to share with the rest of the class in some way.

I would also add here that when it comes to reading for enjoyment, I never ask a learner to finish a book they are not enjoying. It might seem silly, but I have seen it happen, and it can ruin a student's joy of reading. As adults, we wouldn't persevere with a book we hated, so why should we expect our learners to do the same? I am not talking about reading books that we ask the pupils to read as part of a class task, but when it comes to reading for fun, enjoyment of the book they are reading seems a basic requirement for engagement in this area.

There are elements of literacy in everything we do in teaching and learning. If we are not reading or writing, we are listening or talking. So, while there is no shortage of games and activities that can help support and develop specific skills, any play-based activities will involve communication of some kind, whether it be written, read, or spoken.

12 STEAM

STEAM has enjoyed somewhat of a surge in popularity in recent times. The need for STEAM in education came about following a concern that our learners were lacking the critical skills and problem-solving required for the future world of work they would be entering.

Science, Technology, Engineering, Arts, and Mathematics or STEAM is a great vehicle for allowing pupils to develop their skills independently with elements of play. You can use these lesson ideas to focus on something specific you are working on, such as measuring, buoyancy, or natural disasters. I have used lessons like these to develop communication skills by asking mixed groups to work together, assess money and budgeting by asking the groups to 'buy' their resources from me, or building design, engineering, and technology skills by assessing the success of the final item. The focus will depend on your class targets and your teaching objective, and these lessons should be seen as a template for you to build and develop to suit the needs of your learners. And enjoy!

To ensure you include the play element, don't give too many instructions – allow learners to create circular kites, add characters to their zip wires or boats, or add elements to their design that you are sure won't work. Let them learn from trial and error. If you can, don't show them examples or ideas – this will plant images in their minds and prevent them from coming up with their own ideas. You can have some suggestions on standby, though, in case anyone becomes really stuck for ideas. Try to also give them time to sort out any problems, disagreements, or issues they come across. Allowing that time to explore and investigate helps learners understand why certain things work and certain things don't. It feeds into their inquisitiveness and understanding of what they are learning if they can sort it out themselves.

You can also create more of a contextual element by introducing the challenge with a story or context. Each of these lesson ideas comes with a story or context idea, but the great thing about contextual learning and play is that you can adapt this to fit in with a topic you are working on or something that is going on locally. You can start each of these lessons with a design task before you let the class loose on carrying out the task itself, or you can dive straight in. You can also follow up with a review or evaluation lesson, depending on your time available.

The success of the task is easily measured by the learners in seeing how effective their model is at fulfilling the mission you have set for them. You can decide as a class before the start of the task what exactly constitutes success if necessary – time standing or floating, objects it can hold, or whether an item makes it safely to its destination!

DOI: 10.4324/9781003486602-16

96 *Practical Lesson Ideas*

Over time, you can train your class to approach each STEM lesson in the same way. You will present them with a challenge, and they know they will have the freedom to use available resources to come up with a solution creatively. You can decide what resources are appropriate to make available and whether it is best for your class to tackle these challenges independently, in pairs, in groups, or choose for themselves. Create a simple information slide or slide show with the contextual challenge on it and allow your class time to come up with their own solutions to the issue presented to them.

Here are some ideas for activities to get you started, but please remember to adjust and tweak them in any way you see fit for your learners.

Kites

Subject:	STEAM	Area:	Technology, Engineering, Arts
Adult Involvement		●	
Resources:	Paper of various sizes, string, tissue paper, rods, or sticks		
Learning Activity:	Either without showing any examples or showing many examples of different shapes and designs, ask the class to produce a kite with given materials (you can decide which materials and how much). You can deliver this lesson a couple of times using different materials or asking them to create different sized kites and compare their effectiveness in flying.		
	The task will be successful if the kite flies – easy self-assessment!		
	Story/Context: You are required to send a message to a team on the other side of the playground. You need to write the symbol on a kite and fly the kite long enough for the other team to see your message.		

Zip Wires

Subject:	STEAM	Area:	Technology, Engineering
Adult Involvement		● ●	
Resources:	String (or similar such as ribbon), junk, Lego, or similar blocks Something to transport – marbles, tomatoes, eggs!		

STEAM   97

(Continued)

Subject:	STEAM	Area:	Technology, Engineering
Learning Activity:	Create a zip wire to carry a given item from a height to the ground. You can add extra challenge by giving a certain height or length for the zip wire. By bringing in specific measurements, you can add in a mathematical element to the learning as well. Story/Context: You are a palaeontologist, on an archaeological mission. You have uncovered three fossilised dinosaur eggs (marbles or similar items) and must transport them from your mountainside base camp to the science lab at ground level. Design and build a zip wire that will safely carry the eggs from the mountainside (top of your desk) to the base camp on the floor.		

Boats – Sailing or Rafts

Subject:	STEAM	Area:	Science, Engineering
Adult Involvement			
Resources:	Junk, paper, cardboard, tin foil (aluminium foil), lolly sticks, container with water (water tray, paddling pool, etc.), character representations (dolls, Lego/Duplo people, dolly pegs)		
Learning Activity:	Using selected materials, challenge your class to create a vessel that will float on water. You can provide challenges or support with the materials you have available for learners to use and additional specifics, such as creating a raft that will transport a given character or marbles across a stretch of water. Add sails and some wind power to level up their boats. Or challenge them to use a balloon to power their raft. You can also stage a race to add an element of competition! You can add a timing element to determine success (how long can your boat sail for or how long does it take to cross the river?) to incorporate some mathematics, too. Story/Context: You are tasked with transporting a family (Duplo or Lego characters) across a river. They may also have some supplies they need to take with them. It is vital they don't fall in as none of them can swim, and the river is deep. The raft/boat needs to be big enough and strong enough to carry the whole family (and their supplies) across the river safely.		

Figure 12.1 Boat

Pulleys/Cable Cars

Subject:	STEAM	Area:	Technology, Engineering

Adult Involvement

Resources: String, elastic bands, cotton reels (do we still have them lying about?), and various pieces of junk, cards, Lego, K*Nex, or any other construction materials

Learning Activity: For this challenge, use the materials provided to create a pulley or cable car that transports something up (and down if you wish) to a suggested point, such as from the floor to your desk.
Story/Context: Some skiers are trapped at the top of a mountain (your desk). The rescue helicopter is on its way, but it will take a while, and weather conditions mean the skiers are in danger if they don't get supplies of blankets, food, and water soon. You need to create a pulley system or cable car that can transport the supplies safely to the top. (You can provide something to represent the supplies, such as marbles or some Lego pieces).

Parachute

Subject:	STEAM	Area:	Engineering, Science

Adult Involvement

Resources: Plastic bags, tissue paper, cuts of fabric, string, Character (Lego, Duplo, or doll)

Learning Activity: Challenge your learners to select (or buy!) materials that they think will make a good parachute for a given character.
They have a set amount of time to experiment and try out their parachutes with their characters before launch. If you have an upper level in your school, can you parachute the characters from an upstairs window? Success can be measured by how well the parachute glides down.
Story/Context: A pilot needs to eject from his plane during a storm. Create a parachute that will allow him to float to the ground safely.
You can add in a maths element by timing the falls and perhaps declaring the slowest fall as the winner.

Egg Drop Challenge

Subject:	STEAM	Area:	Engineering, Science

Adult Involvement

Resources: Any junk you can find, newspapers, raw eggs

(Continued)

Subject:	STEAM	Area:	Engineering, Science
Learning Activity:	The class designs and creates a system that protects an egg when it is dropped from a height. You may have a window or some playground equipment you can drop it from - outside is preferable! You can limit the resources you offer - only paper plates and straws or paper cups as the starting point. Once complete, you can test the success of the designs by simply placing the eggs in them and dropping them from a height. You can score on imaginative designs, sustainability, and/or survival of the egg. Context/Story: A palaeontologist has discovered some very rare dinosaur eggs on the side of a steep mountain. Your job is to help them transport the egg back to base camp safely.		

Earthquake Simulation

Subject:	STEAM	Area:	Engineering, Technology, Science
Adult Involvement			
Resources:	Junk, blocks, Lego, K*Nex, and other construction materials A board or shakeable table to build models on		
Learning Activity:	Watch some footage of buildings collapsing during an earthquake. Explain that following earthquakes, engineers are often tasked with designing and building constructions that can withstand earthquakes or, at the least, provide more safety than witnessed in the footage shown. Challenge the learners to design and create a building that can withstand an earthquake. To test, shake the table or board on which the buildings are constructed and ask the class to give feedback on the stability of the buildings. Success can be measured by how well the buildings stay up. Context/Story: There has been a terrible earthquake in the town, and the mayor has tasked you with designing safer buildings for the residents. You have limited time to do this, though, as another earthquake has been forecast to hit in an hour (or however long you want to give the task).		

Withstand the Flood

Subject:	STEAM	Area:	Engineering, Technology, Science
Adult Involvement			
Resources:	Junk, blocks, Lego, K*Nex, and other construction materials such as lollipop sticks, play dough, straws, etc. Trays that can hold water		

(Continued)

100 *Practical Lesson Ideas*

(Continued)

Subject:	STEAM	Area:	Engineering, Technology, Science
Learning Activity:	Watch some footage of the effects of flooding – local news, if possible, to make it more relevant. Challenge your learners to design and construct a building that can withstand the effects of a flood. After a given time, test out the creations by standing them in a tray of water (or building them in trays and then pouring water in). Context/Story: Over the past few years, our local area has seen a dramatic rise in rainfall, causing some localised flooding. The local council wants us to design buildings that are flood-proof before the next rainy season begins. We don't have much time, so we need to think fast and design effectively.		

Bridges

Subject:	STEAM	Area:	Engineering, Technology, Science
Adult Involvement			
Resources:	Junk, blocks, Lego, K*Nex, and other construction materials such as lollipop sticks, Play-Doh, paper/card, straws, etc. Toy cars or other vehicles		
Learning Activity:	After looking at some examples of bridges (preferably local ones), discuss and compare the different structures. Give your learners some time to explore bridge structures and investigate their stability in holding given items. Context/Story: The town of Miniville is just across the river from Smalltown. The locals would like to have better transport links between the towns and would like to hire you to design and build a bridge joining the two. Remember, your bridge must be able to stand independently and hold a certain number of cars, as it can get busy at rush hour.		

Figure 12.2 Bridge

Mixtures and Reactions

Subject:	STEAM	Area:	Science

Adult Involvement

Resources: As many materials as you can access – water, oil, coffee powder, sand, soap, washing up liquid, vinegar ...
Containers to mix them in
A recording sheet – depending on ability, you can just provide them with blank paper or a table to record their findings.
If you have them, tuff trays or waterproof coverings for your tables are very useful for this activity. If not, consider doing it outside!

Learning Activity: Give your learners a big but incomplete question such as, "What happens when you mix ... ?"
Provide them with containers, small samples of substances to experiment with, and a sheet to record their findings.
Before you begin, explain the importance of keeping a note of what you are mixing and noting what happens. Give them some vocabulary like dissolve, react, float, sink, combine, absorb, soluble ...
Encourage them to use these words in their notes. If writing is a struggle, perhaps they could record their notes or even film their experiment, providing their own narration.
Allow plenty of time for experimentation and investigation, and enjoy the chaos!

Waterways

Subject:	STEAM	Area:	Engineering, Technology, Science

Adult Involvement

Resources: Paper, tape, water in small containers, such as beakers, to pour and collect water
You can provide additional resources if you choose to – lollipop sticks, straws, cards, etc.

Learning Activity: Provide some input on the Roman water transportation systems. Discuss what forces are required for the water to move from one side to the other (gravity).
Challenge your learners to design and construct a structure using their given resources that will carry water from one side to the other.
Encourage them to consider how their structure will be supported to stand independently and what might happen when you pour water in one end.
Context/Story: Villagers need to collect rainwater and transport it from the hills to their houses. You have been challenged to redesign their aqueduct to carry their water safely. How can you make sure as much water as possible reaches them at the bottom of the hill?

102 *Practical Lesson Ideas*

Scale Models

Subject:	STEAM	Area:	Engineering, Technology, Science, Arts

Adult Involvement

Resources: Card and paper. Scissors, tape, glue
Doll's house with dolls or similar reference points and characters (Duplo is a good size for this)

Learning Activity: Following an input on scale, challenge your learners to create some furniture for the dolls' house - you can describe this as a house or a school, depending on the type of furniture you would like them to create. Encourage them to use the characters to check and compare for scale.

You can extend this by asking them to measure class furniture and devise a scale before creating their own measured desks and chairs.

Context/Story: The tiny family has just moved into their tiny house (or a class has just arrived at their new school). Unfortunately, they don't have any tiny furniture yet. Your challenge is to build them some furniture that will match them - appropriately sized tables, beds, chairs, etc.

Figure 12.3 Scale Models

STEAM 103

Chain Reactions

Subject:	STEAM	Area:	Engineering, Technology, Science

Adult Involvement

Resources: Card, paper, paperclips, Sellotape, string, elastic banks, small junk, marbles, lollipop sticks, straws, K*nex, foil...

Learning Activity: This task can take more than one session so you may need storage to keep each team's resources.

Show your learners some videos of chain reaction systems. There are any number online if you search for 'amazing chain reactions'.

Discuss how chain reactions work and the different ways mechanisms can transfer energy from one system to another.

Learners can be split into teams to create a system of connecting reactions using the materials you have provided them. You can challenge them to create a series of reactions that transport something like a marble from one side of their construction to the other.

Allow the learners time to try out each other's mechanisms to test out how effective they are.

Marble Mazes

Subject:	STEAM	Area:	Engineering, Technology, Science

Adult Involvement

Resources: Paper plates, straws, marbles, Sellotape (double-sided tape might be easier, but more expensive!), scissors

Learning Activity: Challenge your learners to design and build a marble maze on a paper plate. There should be a selection of twists and turns as well as a start and finish point that should be labelled clearly.

Context/Story: The local toy designers are looking for a new type of maze game. They would like a maze that has a variety of twists and turns but has a start and finish point that a marble can navigate through.

You can extend this with a follow-up lesson that challenges learners to create a two-tier marble maze using two paper plates where the marble drops from the top level to the bottom. Or perhaps even higher!

Marble Ramps

Subject:	STEAM	Area:	Engineering, Technology, Science, Maths

Adult Involvement

(Continued)

104 Practical Lesson Ideas

(Continued)

Subject:	STEAM	Area:	Engineering, Technology, Science, Maths
Resources:	Paper, Sellotape, Marbles (As the challenges progress, you may also need paper plates, cards, straws, etc.)		
Learning Activity:	This could be delivered as a series of lessons, getting progressively more challenging as you go. It can also link to maths by measuring the distance of the ramps, timing the marble, and using the data to calculate its speed (Chapter 10). Lesson 1 – Design and build a straight marble ramp on your desk. You must include a marble catcher at the end to prevent it from rolling away. You can add specifics, such as the top of the ramp should be less than 10cm high or the ramp should be at least 20cm long. Lesson 2 – Design and build a J-shaped ramp on your desk. Repeat criteria such as having a marble catcher and/or specifics such as length or height. Lesson 3 – Design and build a U-shaped marble ramp on your desk. Lesson 4 – Design and build a complex marble ramp. It should include at least two straight sections and a curved section. It should take as long as possible for the marble to travel from the start to the finish, but it should travel the entire way independently. You can change the criteria to include more or fewer limitations to their designs.		

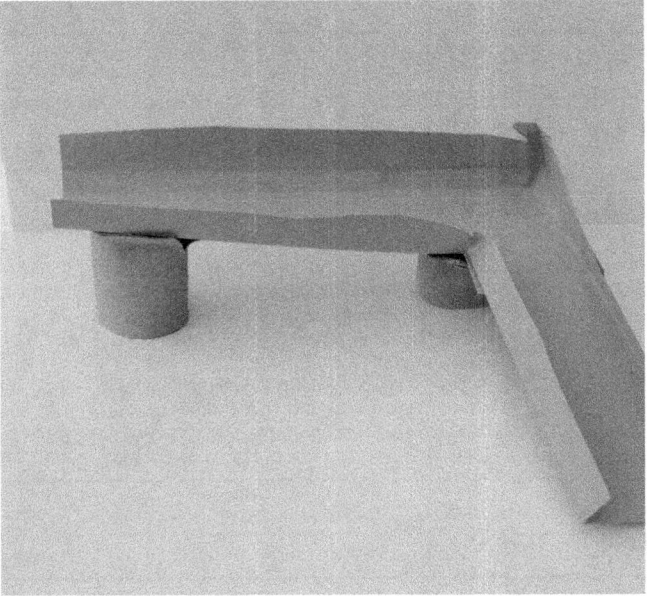

Figure 12.4 Marble Ramp

The Water Cycle

Subject:	Science	Area:	Science
Adult Involvement		● ●	

(Continued)

Subject:	Science	Area:	Science

Resources:	Plastic zip-loc bags (per learner or per group), marker pens, tape
Learning Activity:	This is a good starting point for learning about the water cycle rather than an endpoint, as it invites questioning and wondering BEFORE you teach them about the cycle. If you do it afterwards, they already know what they expect to happen and why it happens, but it does make it real for them.
	Either as individuals or in groups, give your class zip-loc bags and black marker pens to label their bags so they know which are theirs.
	Put a small amount of water into the bags, seal them, and tape them to a window that receives a great deal of sunlight. Ask your learners to keep an eye on their bags and observe what happens. DO NOT tell them what they should expect to see!
	All going well (and with any experiment, it may not for some reason), some students will begin to notice when the water begins evaporating, gathering at the top of the bag and eventually 'raining' back down as it cools.
	You can discuss with them what they think is happening and why, or you can do a lesson on evaporation and precipitation and allow them to make the links. Ask them to illustrate their understanding of the water cycle on their bags – water on the bottom, evaporation caused by the sun, precipitation raining back down.

Inventors

Subject:	STEAM	Area:	Engineering, Technology, Science, History, Arts

Adult Involvement	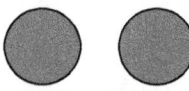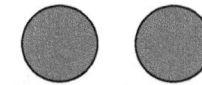
Resources:	Lego, K*nex, Meccano or similar construction material with moving parts
Learning Activity:	Provide learners with input on inventors – this can be linked to a specific theme, such as Victorian inventors, Scottish inventors, female inventors, or inventors who used the wheel, for example.
	Let the input spark a discussion on how inventors see a need for something, a problem that needs to be solved. You can leave it at that and allow your learners some time to design and come up with their own inventions.
	Or you can give them a problem that needs to be solved. Try to make it quite broad and vague to include the principles of play – less teacher-led, more child-led, and allowing learners to have choice as well as motivate and drive themselves.
	Context/Story: You could link this to a particular topic you are doing, or you could create a Dragon's Den-style scenario. Inventors have to present their creations and perhaps even invite your Principal or Headteacher to sit on the panel of Dragons, making their judgements on whether to invest in the new, ground-breaking inventions!

For any of these challenges, you can develop them with a timing element. They must complete the challenge in a specific time, or they can use stopwatches to measure their kite flight/zip wire journey/sailing time, or cable car or marble run journey.

It can also help to have an opportunity for the learners to review each other's work and give them feedback.

You can also add another learning element by having them buy their materials from you. I usually set up a STEAM shop with a range of materials and a price list. Learners or groups are given a budget, say £10, and they must decide what materials they want, need, or can afford to buy to complete their challenge. By creating an interdisciplinary or cross-curricular context, the learning becomes more realistic and credible for your learners.

13 Health and Wellbeing

As mentioned previously, the right to play features in the UN Convention of the Rights of the Child in Article 31. As such, it fits quite nicely into lessons involving health and wellbeing. I have, quite often, given my learners time to simply play following an input on an element of social or emotional health. The main aspects of Health and Wellbeing to consider in teaching are Physical, Social, and Emotional. What follows are some activity ideas for each of these areas.

Physical

Physical Education is a perfect vehicle for providing opportunities for playing games and skill development. Once you have taught a skill and given the pupils some time to practice, it is good to apply these skills in a game situation to create a more sport-like situation. Within PE, there will be opportunities to play games of football, basketball, tennis, and so on, but these activities illustrate some ways to support broader elements like object control or teamwork.

One simple way to include the principles of play into your PE lessons is to involve the learners in planning and teaching activities. Once you have taught the elements of a skill that the class needs, invite them to create their own activities that involve these skills and give them the opportunity to put them into practice. This will also help develop their leadership and organisation skills, and working as part of a group will help their teamwork and communication skills as well.

Ball Skills

These games incorporate elements of throwing, catching, passing, and finding space as well as attacking and defending.

Use Balloons

I can't tell you the number of PE lessons that have become instantly more playful with the introduction of balloons. They make central net (tennis, badminton, volleyball) activities easier and more enjoyable but can also help in other activities such as throwing and catching or balance and coordination.

DOI: 10.4324/9781003486602-17

108   *Practical Lesson Ideas*

Pupils who may have previously struggled now have time to process and move accordingly. The game becomes increasingly more inclusive and fun.

Benchball

Subject:	Health - Physical Ed.	Area:	Ball Skills

Adult Involvement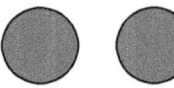

Resources: A ball (basketball, netball, or volleyball is perfect), Bibs, two benches, or marked-out areas for the goalies

In this game, two small-sided teams are split into different halves of the playing area. In this instance, let's say the red team and the blue team with the blues on the left and reds on the right. Each team selects a goalie to stand on a bench in the opposite half. This player essentially acts as a goal or basket. Play can begin from an umpire throw-in or a toss-up with two opposing players battling it out for control of the ball. It is a non-contact sport, and, like netball, there is no movement with the ball. Players must throw the ball to move it around. Once they have released the ball, they are free to move to another position, away from defending opponents. If they succeed in throwing the ball to their 'goalie' on the bench, they get a point for their team. Play begins from the back again, with the goalie passing the ball to an opponent in defence.

The beauty of this game is in its flexibility. As the teacher, you can vary the number of players in each team, the number of passes that must be completed before a shot on goal, the composition of the teams . . . You can change the rules to meet the needs of your class. Goalies can be rotated with every goal scored. You can have a 'key player' who must touch the ball before any shot on goal or make a rule that every player in the team must touch the ball before a shot is made. After a few weeks of playing this game, I usually invite my class to create their own adaptations and teach their new version of the game to their classmates.

Adapted Dodgeball

Subject:	Health - Physical Ed.	Area:	Ball Skills

Adult Involvement

Resources: Dodgeballs or soft balls - netball-sized
Learning Activity: Anyone who has seen the movie of the same name knows the official rules of this sport. In a primary school situation, however, there are several adaptations you can make to the game to make it more suitable for the skills your learners are developing.

Again, you can modify your teams to make it 2 vs 2 or 6 vs 6, whatever works for you. The aim is to hit your opponents below the waist, but you can change this to below the knee for safety reasons or to focus on more specific aiming. Use appropriately soft balls, and you can add rules about the type of throw that you allow in the game - underarm only or only throw with your weaker arm.

I have also been introduced to an adaptation where, instead of being out, hit players stand at the back of the court, behind the opposing team. If their teammates can throw a ball to them, and they catch it, they are allowed back into play. In my opinion, any modification that allows 'out' players back in is a positive. No child should spend part of their PE lesson sitting at the side.

Simplified Versions

There are many ball sports you can modify to create a more playful activity. Remembering that play is chosen, self-motivated, and self-driven, it follows that formal sports, with all the necessary rules, don't quite fit with this description. Unless, of course, the children have chosen the activity and put the rules in themselves! Before moving on to the official rules, why not ask the learners to come up with their own activities that allow some practice of throwing and catching or of passing between players? Offer them some options for balls (various sizes, weights, textures) and allow them to come up with their own game for their classmates to play. You can throw in some additional challenges, such as not moving when you have the ball in your hands, and suddenly, you have the beginnings of a netball game. Or hand keepy uppys with a balloon, with the added challenge that you can't touch the balloon twice in a row, or teams must bat the balloon to opposing sides, and you have the start of a volleyball match.

In my experience with PE, the foundation skills need to be developed and secure before moving on to any type of formal sport. This also allows learners the option of moving between sports. Too often, we come across children who have picked a sport early on (perhaps football/soccer) and, when asked to play rugby or basketball, struggle to transfer the skills. Being more general with the skill development in the beginning allows for more options later. If you consider the motion of an overarm throw, if perfected, this supports an athlete to bowl in cricket, pitch in baseball, serve in tennis, front crawl in the pool, smash in badminton, or throw a javelin. But, teaching a child to throw a javelin does not necessarily mean that they will automatically be able to do the other activities. We need to teach the actions and motions in a more all-purpose manner, and playing games is a great way to do this.

Teamwork

There are not many games you will play in the gym hall that don't require learners to work together. But is this the focus of your lesson? When you focus on teamwork, the actual activity they are being asked to do doesn't have to be sporty. Why not try some of these activities to build some teamwork skills while you have the space to do so? These activities can be done in a gym hall, empty classroom, or outside.

The Floor is Lava

Subject:	Health – Physical Ed.	Area:	Teamwork
Adult Involvement		● ●	
Resources:	Gym mats or other equipment such as balance pods, wooden balance planks, plastic trail sections, etc.		

(Continued)

(Continued)

Subject:	Health – Physical Ed.	Area:	Teamwork
Learning Activity:	In groups, the children have to get from one side of the hall to the other without anyone's feet touching the floor. In a twist on the well-known game, they can use whatever equipment you have provided for them to use, but the task is only successful when everyone makes it safely to the other side. Resist the urge to suggest ways to do it or demonstrate how they should do it beforehand. One of the joys of playing is trying out different things to see what works and, inevitably, what doesn't.		

Ball Carry

Subject:	Health – Physical Ed.	Area:	Teamwork
Adult Involvement			
Resources:	Large balls (1 per team) or other items the team must transport		
Learning Activity:	In small groups, children have to carry a large ball from one side of the hall to the other without using their hands. Or they have to transport the ball (or other piece of equipment, such as a hoop or box) from one side to the other, with everyone in the team touching the item. You can make this a simple challenge or a race between teams, and you can modify it by adding equipment they need to transport or changing the number of people in each group.		

Hoop Pass

Subject:	Health – Physical Ed.	Area:	Teamwork
Adult Involvement			
Resources:	Large hoop – one per team		
Learning Activity:	This can be done in small groups or as a whole class. Pupils join hands, either in a line or a circle. Place a hoop over one child's arm, and the challenge is to move the hoop around the circle or to the end of the line without breaking the chain. You can time the class completing the activity to see how fast they can get or split the class into two groups and have a race.		

These teamwork activities are also a great way to start your year, building relationships and showing your class how they can work together well.

Balance and Coordination

Once you have gone over the main aspects of balance and coordination, introducing additional elements such as rotation, inversion, or counterbalancing, the next step might be to create routines or sequences. This is where your play principles can come into play. Give your learners the freedom to create their own routines, including elements they choose to include. Allow their opportunities to be intrinsically motivated by encouraging them to create a routine that they can present to their peers. You can make it even more playful with some scoring or peer feedback.

These routines can be across some floor mats or with some equipment. I always find it a good idea to show the class some Olympic-level gymnastics to give them inspiration. I certainly would never be able to demonstrate the moves of a rhythmic or floor gymnast that would inspire a class of 11-year-olds to create their own routines!

Balance Cards

Subject:	Health – Physical Ed.	Area:	Balance and Coordination

Adult Involvement

Resources:	Image cards representing parts of the body
Learning Activity:	Have a series of image cards representing parts of the body – one foot, one hand, two feet, one elbow, etc. Ask groups to pick a few cards and create a balance using these body parts, either individually or collectively. Or use the cards as a warm-up. Have the class walk or run around the hall. On a shout of STOP, hold up a card. Everyone must place that or those body parts on the floor.

Dice Balance

Subject:	Health – Physical Ed.	Area:	Balance and Coordination

Adult Involvement

Resources:	Large Dice
Learning Activity:	Use a dice (a large, inflatable, or foam one is ideal for the gym hall, but small ones will also do). Groups or individuals roll the dice to determine how many body parts should touch the ground for a given balance. Landing on one might see a balance on one foot, but the more coordinated might manage a headstand, so try not to tell the class what body parts to balance on. You could also use dice in another way. Display the numbers 1-6 with corresponding body parts, shapes, or balances, ideally discussed and agreed with the input of the class.

E.g.:
1- Solo balance on one body part
2- Paired balance – mirror a balance with a partner
3- Symmetrical Balance – where both the left and right sides of your body are doing the same thing
4- Counterbalance involving two people
5- Dynamic balance – a moving balance
6- An inverted balance – a balance where at least a part of your body is upside down

Roll the dice and follow the instructions accordingly, again, either independently or as part of a group.

112   *Practical Lesson Ideas*

Social

These activities are designed to support teaching and learning in social health areas.

Board Games

Subject:	Health	Area:	Social Wellbeing
Adult Involvement		● ●	
Resources:	Board games – Chess, Draughts/Checkers, Connect 4, Dobble, Jigsaw Puzzles, any other games you have to hand.		
Learning Activity:	Board Games are such a simple yet very effective way to encourage social skills and cooperation. You could start each term with some time to play in teams on a board game. There are many board games that also lend themselves to more curricular links as well, such as Game of Life (money), Scrabble (spelling), or Taboo (vocabulary).		
	I often use board games to teach my class about mathematical thinking and strategy. Many games, such as Connect 4 (4 in a row), Chess, or Checkers (Draughts), are great for thinking ahead and planning steps and potential moves. This can lead nicely to some computational thinking and coding if you are teaching these skills as well.		

Setting your learners some co-operative challenges can encourage teamwork as well as develop vital life skills such as communicating, negotiating, and problem-solving. Challenge them to build a Lego tower with alternate players having to place bricks or each player only having certain bricks (player 1 has the squares, player 2 has the rectangles or something similar).

As their teacher, you should, of course, intervene if there is an element of safety being compromised or learners are struggling to stay on task, but as much as possible, allow them to sort out their own arguments, solve their own problems, and learn how to win or lose graciously.

New Partners

Subject:	Health	Area:	Social Wellbeing
Adult Involvement		● ●	
Resources:	Paper, pencils		
Learning Activity:	This activity encourages learners to work with different people and build that ability to work with those they wouldn't normally work with.		
	Leave the paper and the pencils out on the desks. Play some music and have the pupils walk around the room – encourage them to change directions and use the space well.		

(Continued)

Subject:	Health	Area:	Social Wellbeing

Stop the music. Everyone must sit in the nearest available seat. Ask them to complete a short challenge with the person next to them. Depending on your seating arrangements, this might be the person opposite them or their shoulder partner, but you deliver the instructions in a way that ensures everyone is working with someone.

The youngest of the pair should draw a head and the partner should add in some eyes (or something similar). You then start the music, and everyone moves again, leaving their unfinished picture on the desk.

Stop the music and repeat with another instruction (you may need to add a condition that you cannot sit next to someone you have just worked with) - the oldest in the pair should add a nose to the drawing that is in front of them, and the partner adds a mouth.

Repeat as many times as you feel is suitable for your class.

I have found that as the learners realise the task is very short and easy, they quickly give up complaining about who they are sitting next to or trying to sit next to their friends!

You can modify this activity by changing the item that is to be drawn or adding conditions to the challenge - draw with your non-dominant hand, draw whatever your partner tells you to, or close your eyes and your partner delivers instructions.

No Instructions

Subject:	Health	Area:	Social Wellbeing

Adult Involvement

Resources: Large rolls of paper (leftovers from backing paper are perfect); other classroom resources - scissors, pens, tape, etc.

Learning Activity: Sometimes, the simplest of activities can facilitate a whole bundle of learning opportunities and experiences.

Give your class leftover backing paper from wall displays (the stuff that comes in rolls and you know won't be used by another teacher!). Simply hand out the large pieces of paper and leave the pupils to work out what they can do with it. Do not give them any instructions or ideas. You may need to explain or write "No Instructions Given" on the board to give them a clue as to what is expected of them.

I tried this at the end of the year with a class of P6s (Year 5s). By the end of the session, we had a giant Twister game, a pirate's treasure map, a light sabre, and a "doodle table" (paper covering the desk and everyone drawing all over it!). Once we tidied up, all the paper was recycled, and the class had some great stories to share with their peers and families.

I have done a similar activity with old cardboard boxes. The key is to give the class little to no instructions. Allow them to be creative and try out some different things. Try not to interfere! Ask questions ("What is this you're building? What are you planning to do with this? Have you come across any tricky issues?") and answer any questions they may have. Although, try a few "What do you think?" type responses before you give them solutions to any problems they come across.

Emotional

These are some activity ideas for supporting teaching and learning around emotional health and wellbeing.

Expressionism

Subject:	Health	Area:	Emotional Wellbeing

Adult Involvement

Resources: Paper, paint, crayons, pastels, pencils – any art materials you have handy and are happy for your class to use

Learning Activity: Art can be a great way to express yourself. Look at some examples of expressionism and discuss with your class the emotions and feelings that they generate. Discuss the features that make this possible, such as showing emotion in a picture – the colours, the lines, and the picture itself.

You now have a tool to allow your learners to express themselves in quite a free way.

When you ask them to create their own piece of artwork as part of an emotional health activity, allow free choice as much as you can. Don't ask them to replicate the work of another artist; this would not allow them to express themselves. If you are able to do so, have no restrictions on the materials, resources, or methods they can use to create their artwork. Don't comment on the artistic skills either. Discuss the emotions and how they felt as they were painting or how they feel about their work now that it is complete.

You can ask the class for feedback on their peers' work or create a gallery for others to visit.

Talking Time

Subject:	Health	Area:	Emotional Wellbeing

Adult Involvement

Resources: None

Learning Activity: As children grow, they have changing challenges, concerns, and worries. Giving them time to talk gives them an opportunity to share these thoughts with others.

Create a safe space for learners to share their experiences, their worries, and their ideas, and you will create an environment that the children feel part of. Set aside time to talk to the class as a group or with individuals.

Give them time to talk to each other as well. It can sound impossible in a curriculum that is already so busy, but ten minutes on a Monday morning to discuss how everyone's weekend has been or the last 10 minutes on a Friday to find out what everyone's favourite part of the week has been can go far. I have had a 'Bubble Box' in my class for learners to post notes for me or ask for 1 to 1 time to chat about something.

(Continued)

Subject:	Health	Area:	Emotional Wellbeing

More recently, I set up a QR code for the class to access an online form they can discreetly send me to tell me if something is on their mind. It comes with two options – "I want to chat to you about this" or "I just want you to know".

Either way, the pupils know they can tell me things without judgement and†I will listen, and the class loves it. By creating time for your class to†talk, you are showing that you will listen, and if you show action based on their thoughts and ideas, they are more likely to contribute further.

Story Time

Subject:	Health	Area:	Emotional Wellbeing

Adult Involvement

Resources: Storybook or novel

Learning Activity: As a grown adult, I still enjoy listening to an audiobook, so I think you are never too old to listen to a story. Although it is tempting to move on to class novels as the children get older, I have taught many 12-year-olds who love listening to a good picture book! I often use story time as an opportunity to just wind down and relax but it can often lead to many further learning activities. As mentioned earlier, a good rhyming book can produce some great rhyming work from the class, and similarly, a funny book or one with a twist at the end can inspire them to want to create their own.

Quiet Time

Subject:	Health	Area:	Emotional Wellbeing

Adult Involvement

Resources: None – but you might choose to have something to display a timer on or play relaxing music or a mindfulness activity

Learning Activity: Take some time to do nothing.

It sounds so strange for us as teachers, as we are so used to cramming a lot of stuff into our days and making sure our learners get through all of the work we give them successfully. But this is exhausting.

It is just as important to show our learners that it is ok to just do nothing every now and then.

You will know your own learners, so use your professional judgement on what will work best for them. Some classes love ten minutes of complete silence. Some find this unnerving and very difficult to sit through.

(Continued)

(Continued)

Subject:	Health	Area:	Emotional Wellbeing
	I sometimes provide scrap paper and pencils on tables while we have quiet time, play sleep music, or have a candle or fireplace video on the whiteboard for them to look at while we relax. You can also find lots of mindfulness activities online that go through breathing exercises or body scans that allow us to focus on ourselves for a time. Get feedback from the class about what works for them and which activities helped them the most.		
	No matter what the activity, I would say a categorical NO TALKING during this quiet time. Keep it as short as you need to, but sometimes, learning how to be quiet is a more difficult skill to develop than learning to chat.		

14 Other Subject Areas

In this section, I have tried to show how the play principles can be applied to the way you approach learning and teaching in general. There are some lesson examples to demonstrate how this might look, but they are illustrative examples designed to inspire you to try them or create your own lessons that meet your planning needs.

Show Your Learning in Different Ways

When you are finished teaching a particular concept or topic, do you look for written assessment results to demonstrate the learners' understanding, or are there other ways they can show what they have learned?

Here are a couple of examples in which a written report or assignment might be an option for some learners, but an alternative is also available.

Land Formation

Subject:	Social Studies	Area:	Geography
Adult Involvement		● ●	
Resources:	Junk, newspapers, glue, (paper mâché), Play-Doh, clay, modelling clay, or similar		
Learning Activity:	After learning about how particular land features are or were formed, learners are given the option of writing a report or step-by-step explanation text with diagrams or creating a 3D representation of the feature using a choice of materials.		
	Allow your learners the autonomy to select how they are going to demonstrate their learning about the land feature. They could create their models with junk or clay, paint it or leave it plain, vary its size – if they can describe the features to you, they are showing their learning in a context.		
	Once completed, you can showcase the models alongside any written work completed, explaining the features or how the land was formed. However you decide to show it off, the application of their learning into a more active lesson will help your learners deepen their understanding and explain it to others.		

(Continued)

DOI: 10.4324/9781003486602-18

118 *Practical Lesson Ideas*

(Continued)

Subject:	Social Studies	Area:	Geography
	Building models can show an understanding of land formation or how land has changed over time. You could challenge them further to show their understanding of how rivers move or how mountains are formed. Step-by-step models or drawings, stop motion animations, comic strips – any of these can give you the information you need about your students' understanding without you dictating exactly what they need to do. The element of choice allows for the element of play.		

Weather

Subject:	Science/Social Studies	Area:	Science/Geography/Weather
Adult Involvement	● ●		
Resources:	Digital devices for filming, props or backgrounds, map of your country or local area		
Learning Activity:	When learning about the weather, why not create your own weather report? Perhaps make it part of a bigger project on the news, but the weather report will create an opportunity for lots of vocabulary and discussion about how to communicate information about the weather to others. This could be a written report or one suitable for TV. The more confident your students could take on the role of the weather reporter, talking through the forecast and what that means for your local residents, while your less confident individuals could be part of the research team, scriptwriters, map creators, or even camera crew. If videoing isn't an option, a radio weather report is just as useful in showing what the class has been learning about and how they can link it to their own lives.		

Art

Art is a fantastic opportunity to allow pupils to express themselves and show their creativity in unique ways unless you teach your art lessons with full control and demonstrations that lead to 30 versions of the same piece of artwork. While I can see how this clearly demonstrates to anyone asking that everyone has met the success criteria of your lesson, I can't help but think the success criteria of an art lesson can still be met when the learners implement the play principles to complete their own unique piece of art.

Art is the go-to activity for many teachers when they need to do something creative with their learners. But art by itself is not necessarily a creative activity if, as mentioned previously, you consider an art lesson where the learning intention is related to the recognition of detail. You could model a lesson on drawing a bowl of fruit you have displayed, emphasising the shapes, proportions, shadows, and then provide the class with their paper to produce 25 pictures of a bowl of fruit from different angles. Or a lesson where you look at the work of Picasso, discussing the abstract nature of his work and cubism. You show them the painting of the "Weeping Woman" as an example and then instruct them to paint their own portrait in Picasso's Cubist style.

In each of these examples, you will inevitably end up with around 30 pieces of very similar artwork. I often see teachers sharing their class's artwork on social media, and while I admire the application of a given technique or method, I'm often struck by the missing element of creativity and individualism in the different pieces.

Instead, consider whether these art lessons would work with your learners to teach a given outcome but also include some creativity and play.

Attention to Detail

Subject:	Art	Area:	Attention to Detail

Adult Involvement ● ●

Resources: Examples of artwork demonstrating detail, art resources (paints, pastels, crayons, pencils, chalk, charcoal), paper
*sidebar - the more resources you can offer learners to choose from, the more playful the learning becomes and the more creative they can be

Learning Activity: Show the class a range of artwork displaying detail, emphasising shape, proportion, shadow, and colours but from a range of styles using a range of materials (Michaelangelo, Dali, van Gogh, and the ancient Egyptian hieroglyphs all contain a lot of detail in their artwork).
Now recap the importance of the detail elements and allow your learners to create their own artwork. This could be on a given theme (landscapes or castles) or a representation of a given item (the classic bowl of fruit or vase of flowers!).

Styles of Painting

Subject:	Art	Area:	Styles of Painting

Adult Involvement ● ●

Resources: Powerpoint or display showing examples of some famous artwork (Picasso's Weeping Woman for Cubism, Dali's The Persistence of Memory for Surrealism, Munch's The Scream for Expressionism)

Learning Activity: Show the class some famous artwork, describing the different styles as you go.
Invite discussion and share opinions. I always explain to my class that there are pieces of art that sell for hundreds of thousands of pounds that I wouldn't want hanging in my living room. I am a big fan of Dali's work, whereas others find it too weird. It's important for learners to realise that every art style is not going to appeal to everyone, and that is okay. We discuss our preferences or any piece of art that stands out to us.
Then, invite the class to choose a style that appeals to them and paint something for the class gallery. Have them label their work with their name, title of their work, and what style they had chosen. Invite your class to present their work, explaining why they chose the style they did, whether they were inspired by any particular artist or style of art. Encourage learners to give each other feedback on the work - model polite criticism ("This style isn't to my particular taste, but I love how you have used the colours to show emotion"). Now you have some very different pieces of art to showcase and students who are able to discuss different styles of art as well as their own preferences confidently.

Expressionism

Subject:	Art/Health and Wellbeing	Area:	Emotions Artistic Styles

Adult Involvement

Resources: Examples of artwork demonstrating expressionism, art resources (paints, pastels, crayons, pencils, chalk, charcoal), paper

Learning Activity: Show the class a range of expressionist art and explain that the movement occurred at the beginning of the 20th Century. The aim of the artists was to express emotion rather than physical reality.
Look at some examples and discuss which emotions the artists might have been trying to convey. You might need to list some emotions beforehand, depending on prior work on emotional literacy. Highlight that there might be different answers, as art is open to interpretation.
Now, invite your class to consider an emotion and create a piece of artwork that represents this. Ask them to give it a title linked to the emotion.

I am reminded of a very thought-provoking poem by Helen E. Buckley about a little boy who is told what to do and how to do it so often by his teachers that he loses his own creativity. It is called "The Little Boy", if you want to look it up. It made such an impact on me when I read it, and it really hit home how important it is to not make creativity and art about ourselves and what we would like to see but more about the learners applying the techniques we teach them to their own special creations. It is one of the reasons I have not included any pictures in this book of the work produced by my learners during play activities. I don't want to create an image of how your learners' play *should* look. It will look however it looks. Every child is different; their learning experiences are different, and their pathways are different. As such, their work should all look different. If you end up with 25 pieces of art that all look the same, then your class has achieved success in copying but not necessarily applying skills in an individual and independent context.

History

If you can link history to today, it will make the learning more meaningful for your students – looking at how certain wars shaped the population of our community or the laws introduced in the past that are still used today – but one way to include play in lessons involving history is in the use of imaginative play. Create some role-play opportunities where the class can act out the tactics of a battle or make some decisions if you were the king/president/prime minister at a given period in history.

A former class of mine can still recall the basics of William Wallace's tactics during the Battle of Stirling Bridge, as he shepherded the English army towards the river so the only way they could progress was across a narrow bridge. The Scottish army simply waited at the other side of the bridge and took the soldiers out in smaller numbers. My teaching technique for this? Tell the story of the battle, then ask the learners to create a model depicting the scene, showing how Scotland won the battle. The application of their knowledge was shown through Lego models, wooden blocks, junk modelling, Play-Doh, and drawings. As they explained their work to me, I knew they had understood the strategy perfectly.

Religious and Moral Education

Any teaching involving religion, beliefs, and morals allows a lot of opportunity for play principles to be brought in. Our beliefs are so personal to us. Give your learners the opportunity to express their feelings, beliefs, and understanding of religion in a safe space. If you teach in a faith school, you will obviously be guided by the standards of your school or curriculum, but how you involve your class in their learning or allow them to express their thoughts and understanding of their faith might be a bit more flexible.

Understanding and beliefs will develop as learners grow and mature. If we can provide a safe and engaging space for them to explore this, then that is a privilege.

Some activities I have enjoyed with my classes since embracing the play principles into my teaching recently are:

> Painting stones to show what they love about our world. This could be linked to reflections on a specific origins story or nature aspect as we consider our world and everything about it.

Reflecting on religious stories and retelling in a choice of ways. I have asked pupils to consider the Bible story that means the most to them and create a representation of that story. You can do this through a comic strip, poster, tableau, or song – the element of choice is what creates the play aspect, and this can be used to share personal views of a specific story, whether it be religious or moral or their choice of story from a selection you have shared and discussed.

Take a passage, perhaps some scripture or a well-known prayer. Often, these are written in a style that is unfamiliar to our young learners. Can they reflect on the important message of the passage and write it in a way that will resonate more with their peers?

Religious Education is a tricky area to make modifications to, but if you can make it link directly to the lives of your learners and create an environment that invites discussion and debate, you have created a playful classroom for these lessons to take place.

Digital Technologies

Depending on where you are teaching, your access to digital technologies may vary, but they can be a very useful tool for differentiating and supporting differing learner needs. Using individual devices, handheld games consoles, or a shared interactive screen, the play principles come into action when we allow learners the freedom to use their skills in their own ways. Block-building games like Minecraft allow learners to use their creativity, and if you choose to give them a specific task, try to make it open-ended and allow space for individual interpretations. For example, "using what we've learned, create a world that shows how the Romans lived" is much more open than "create a Roman house with pillars and three rooms".

Plenty of websites have curriculum-themed games that can support learning, spelling, mathematical concepts, number processes, writing, and so on; just check that they support your taught strategies and methods. You can also use online quiz sites to create learning quizzes or have your learners create their own.

The online world also provides us with a great opportunity to allow learners to find things out for themselves in a safe environment in which you can question their findings. Are you sure that's factual? How can we make sure?

We can also use digital technology to support our learners. Giving learners the option to type instead of write, produce a slide presentation instead of a report, or film themselves giving a verbal account of something are all valuable ways of recording learning that gives learners an element of control and choice.

Playful Learning Activities

There are certain lesson formats you can take and adapt to meet the learning needs of your class. We are all familiar with the pedagogy of teaching from the board and having students complete a given task or perhaps setting out stations of activities for the class to complete in groups, but here are some other formats for lessons that are playful but also help with retrieval of learning and development of skills and application.

In any subject where you are asking students to learn facts, dates, or specific information, it can be quite tricky to use play to teach this. When supporting memorisation and recall, however, play can be crucial to keeping them engaged.

Create quizzes about your given subject, or better still, invite the class to create their own flashcards, quiz questions, or games to help their classmates recall the information you have taught them.

Format	Potential Curricular Areas	Lesson
Quizzes	Social Studies, History, Geography, Numeracy, Science	Host a quiz about your given subject. You can break it into rounds, scoring at the end of each, or better still, find a website like Kahoot that allows you to score live and see the results. I have often used this method to check prior knowledge before starting a topic and then assessing by hosting the same quiz at the end of a block. You can adapt the quiz to be in the style of a particular gameshow to raise engagement and enjoyment while learning and recalling facts.
Escape Room	Physical Education, Social Studies, Numeracy/Maths	Set the class a challenge to complete a number of tasks before they can 'exit' the room. These can be problem-solving, fact recall, or physical challenges, depending on the learning that you want them to develop. Learners complete their challenge sheet with the correct answers, adequate working or physical completion, and present their work to you to be allowed to exit.
Game Show	Literacy, Numeracy, Physical Education	As mentioned previously, you can host a gameshow with a quiz element to recall facts, but you can also develop a different gameshow aspect. Shows like Gladiators or The Crystal Maze have physical elements that you can adapt into Physical Education lessons, or shows like Lingo or Countdown have obvious curricular links to Literacy or Numeracy.

(Continued)

Format	Potential Curricular Areas	Lesson
Board Games	Numeracy, Literacy, Health and Wellbeing, Critical Thinking, Strategy, etc.	Monopoly and Game of Life are classics for numeracy, while Scrabble, Boggle, and Taboo all help develop literacy skills. Games like Connect 4, Chess, and Draughts help develop forward-thinking and strategy, not to mention the teamwork, communication, negotiating, resilience, and other social and meta-skills that are being developed. There are countless other games that could be listed here, too.
Sequences	Literacy, Numeracy, Social Studies (History, Geography, Modern/Political Studies)	Have a selection of cards with words, events, numbers, or pictures on them. In pairs or groups, learners need to put the cards in a particular order. It can be used to put numbers in ascending or descending order, important events in chronological order, or process stages into a particular sequence (think life cycle of a butterfly or stages of the water cycle). If you are in a position to do this electronically, then it makes the whole process easier to organise as you don't need many copies of your resources; you only need to share it.
Matching Activities	Literacy, Numeracy, Social Studies	As the name suggests, this activity simply involves matching items together. This could be matching synonyms together, matching words with pictures, or matching percentages with fractions – whatever meets your learning target.

15 Project-Based Learning

As teachers, we are often programmed to be in control. It's probably in our DNA. As a result, letting go of some of that control can be daunting. Nevertheless, it can also be so rewarding.

Project-based learning gives learners a context to develop skills such as researching, learning about the reliability of sources, carrying out their own experiments or investigations, referencing their sources, taking notes, turning these notes into something new, and presenting them to others. You can allow them to choose a topic that interests them or select from a list (helpful when trying to engage learners), and you can allow them to choose how they present their learning at the end. A recent P7 (Year 6) class of mine chose to organise a showcase for their families, and a walk around the stalls revealed posters, interactive quizzes, PowerPoints, and accompanying music and lights. The pupils were so engaged and invested in showing off their learning that the projects needed very little from me other than obtaining the resources they needed for their final presentations.

The main differences between project-based learning and traditional learning are:

Project-Based	Traditional
Student-led	Teacher-led
Contextual and real	Abstract and theoretical
The outcome of the project drives the teaching; the curriculum can be flexible and fit around the project	The curriculum is fixed and followed absolutely
The learning is more active	The learning is more passive
There is an emphasis on problem-solving and critical thinking skills	The emphasis is on memorising facts and repeating them
Achievement is measured by the successful outcome of the project	Achievement is measured using standardised tests for all
Teamwork, sharing ideas, and working together is encouraged	There is more of a focus on individual achievement

Project-based learning can take different forms. As the teacher, you can give the class a project to work towards. In my current school, the oldest class organises a coffee morning to raise money for charity. I know of many others who organise fundraising events or enterprise projects as a class. This whole-class thematic learning can incorporate any number of curricular areas. In our Coffee Morning example, I taught lessons on money, calculating totals, and finding change as well as profit and loss. We also did some work on advertising and persuasive language to promote the event, as well as letter writing and sending emails to various companies for donations. Afterwards, we reflected on the success of the event, looking at our profits and doing some Social Health work on how the money we made might be used by the charity we supported. I also allowed the class some flexibility in where they took these lessons, following class discussions about the coffee morning and learning a little about working in the world of retail.

Other projects could be more child-led (embracing even more of a play aspect). They can be short-term activities or longer-term ventures. An example of a short-term project would be inviting the learners to complete a task that interests them – building a car from Lego, reading more about the Egyptians, or making a birthday card for a family member.

A longer-term project could be more research or engineering-based. Finding out about the Titanic or developing a water transportation system. This could be done over a few lessons or a few weeks.

The key to the success of these project-based learning opportunities is to allow time to plan, do, and review their projects. As with the APDR record of tests of change mentioned earlier, for us to see the impact of an activity, we need to plan it, do it, review it, and assess its success. You can ask learners to review their own activity, explaining what they set out to do and how they got on, or you can invite peers to assess the success of each other's project. Either way, the review element presents some accountability, and while the elements of play still exist, the purpose you give their play ensures that they have meaningful experiences and skills that transfer into later years and adulthood.

This is not a return to topic-based learning of the past, where we announce to the class what the topic is, tell them what they are going to learn, and show them where to find the answers to the questions we set. This is a more flexible and pupil-led approach.

I recently invited my Primary 7 (Year 6) class to complete a five-week independent research project. We spent the first week just thinking about the topics. What were we interested in? What did we want to find out about it? How could we find out?

I also gave them a choice in how they wanted to present their research for a showcase we were going to hold at the end of term, inviting parents and families, the headteacher, depute head and other visitors we wanted to show off to. Learners could choose to present their work in a report, a poster, a PowerPoint, or a presentation of some kind.

Over the course of the five weeks, I observed and supported projects about the Titanic, World War II, Celtic Football Club, Taylor Swift, Hello Kitty, Stephen King's *IT*, Little Mix, and the History of the Flag of the USA. Presentations included interactive quizzes, videos, flashing lights, music, interactive posters with pictures, lifting flaps, and red balloons handed out to our younger visitors. Some worked with peers, but most chose to work alone.

It was, by far, one of the most fun series of lessons I have ever taught. Every learner researched, took notes, questioned the reliability of their sources, learned something new, and presented their learning in a way that was inviting, attractive, and informative for our visitors. They were proud of their work. They were keen to show it off. It was theirs.

126 Practical Lesson Ideas

Ideas for Projects

Class Garden

Curricular Areas:	Science, Social Studies,
Adult Involvement	
Resources:	Seeds, pots Other gardening equipment if you have it - watering cans, gloves, mini trowels, etc.
Learning Activity	If you have an area of the school grounds that can be used for this, that is great. If not, you can create an indoor garden within the classroom. Have your class research appropriate plants for growing in their given area - space needed, growing conditions, and care needed. Give them the seeds and any other resources required and leave it up to them. Have them be responsible for their own plants, and apart from checking in with them and allowing them time to care for their plants, step back and let them learn from their gardening experience. You could have them write instructions for caring for plants or an experiment report, placing the plants in different conditions.

Park Design

Subject:	STEM	Area:	Engineering, Technology, Maths, Art
Adult Involvement			
Resources:	Junk, blocks, Lego, K*Nex, other construction materials such as lollipop sticks, Play-Doh, string, paper/card, straws, etc.		
Learning Activity:	Discuss some local park areas and the kind of equipment you can find there. Make a bank of ideas that the class can draw on in their own designs. The class has to redesign a local park with ideas for different areas of the park and different equipment. Have a character or a doll that you can use as a size reference and link to measure and scale. The first task is to design the park on paper - create a boundary for the park and/or different areas with some perimeter work and safe ground coverings using area. Challenge the class to design and create a piece of equipment for the park. You can decide if you want to limit the choice so you have one of each item or if you don't mind having five swings and a slide! Using the construction materials that you provide for them, learners create their park equipment and combine their creations to eventually construct a class park.		

(Continued)

Subject:	STEM	Area:	Engineering, Technology, Maths, Art

Figure 15.1 Lego Park

Action Against Pollution/Energy Waste

Curricular Areas:	Science, Social Studies, Health, Maths (data handling)
Adult Involvement	
Resources:	Internet, Presentation materials (PowerPoint, poster paper, Google slides)
Learning Activities	Discuss the concept of pollution or energy waste, types of pollution, and the potential effects on the environment with your class. Link it to your local area and specifically your school. In groups, learners can research chosen types of pollution or waste and create an action plan to tackle the problem in their classroom, school, or local community. Perhaps present their plans to the headteacher or at a school assembly. If possible, support them in carrying out their plan and find ways to measure the positive impact their plan makes.

128   *Practical Lesson Ideas*

Class Economy

Curricular Areas:	Numeracy (Financial Education), Social Studies, Health, and many others, depending on your class
Adult Involvement	
Resources:	Spreadsheet or similar to keep track of finances, various other resources depending on 'businesses'
Learning Activity	Establish a class currency - school bucks, Imagipounds - anything your class decides on.
	Then, decide on an earning strategy. I would start with something as simple as £10 (you could also design your own currency sign!) for completing their work each day.
	Input all the learners' names into a spreadsheet or similar, along with their income, to keep track of their balance. They may want to check how much 'money' they have during the week!
	After a week or so, you can introduce expenditures like rent or utilities, and pupils can perhaps earn extra income by doing their homework or completing additional tasks - always make these rewards based on effort, not performance.
	You can then introduce some things that the class can 'spend' their money on - choosing the music on a Friday afternoon, hiring out a cushion to sit on, etc.
	If you have the time, you could extend it to having your learners set up their own businesses. I have had nail bars, Minecraft festivals, hair salons, fortune telling stalls, cleaning companies . . . each charging their classmates a few 'bucks' to partake of their service. They take appointments, organise their business and keep note of their transactions, which they then pass on to the bank (me!) to be inputted into their accounts. I have hired pupils to run the bank once they get the hang of the system.
	I have challenged learners further by introducing company shares, which pupils can sell to each other. They then eagerly check each Monday morning to see if their shares have gone up, by how many percent, and how much their company is worth now!

Board Games

Curricular Areas:	Technology/Any other curricular areas of your choice
Adult Involvement	
Resources:	Cardboard, paper, pens, dice, counters
Learning Activity	Have a look at some board games. Maybe spend some time playing them. Discuss what we enjoyed about the games and what wasn't so good. Create a list of what makes a good board game.
	Task your learners with designing and creating their own board game. You can give it a focus (using money in some way, quiz questions on a given category, risk, and forfeits), or you can give them free rein. You can have them write out the instructions for the game and perhaps design a box to hold it all.
	Once the games are completed, share them with each other, or better yet, share them with people outside of the class - invite another class to play or invite families in for a game afternoon.
	You can adapt this further by creating digital games. If you have access to devices and the know-how, you can challenge your learners to code or provide written instructions for a multi-player interactive game.

Cafe

Curricular Areas:	*Technology; Health; Mathematics*

Adult Involvement	
Resources:	Ingredients for preparing foods of your choice
Learning Activity	Create a class cafÈ, offering snacks or food to other classes or staff.
	This can be as simple as a toast or fruit cafÈ, but it can become as fancy and as wide-ranging as you have the capacity for.
	Have the learners plan out everything – how they are going to fund the venture (can you give them a starting fund?)? How much will they need to make to be able to keep the cafÈ going? How much will they need to charge their customers? How are they going to advertise the cafÈ? How will it be staffed?
	Review it with them regularly and link to learning wherever you can – money, profit and loss, persuasive language, health, and wellbeing.

Fashion Show

Curricular Areas:	*Technology;*

Adult Involvement	
Resources:	Old clothes, sewing materials, stationery (paperclips, stapler, etc.)
Learning Activity	Challenge your learners to organise and present a fashion show.
	Depending on the time you have available for this project, you could have them schedule the fashion show, organise the location, send out invitations, create a programme for the event, organise a running order and runway music.
	They also need to design and create new outfits using the old clothes and model them at the runway event.
	You can link this to any work the school might be doing on recycling, sustainability, global goals, and eco-schools.

Publish a Book

Curricular Areas:	*Literacy; Art;*

Adult Involvement	
Resources:	Cardboard, paper, pens, dice, counters
Learning Activity	Why not use a self-publishing site to publish a book of short stories written by your class? Or even school.
	As mentioned previously, there are various ways to self-publish online, but you could also support your learners in creating an eBook that they can share electronically through email, your school website, or any online platform your school uses to share learning.

16 Continuous Provision

Continuous provision refers to resource and learning areas that are available all of the time within your learning environment. When set up and developed well, it will encourage children to interact, investigate, explore, and inevitably learn independently. When used effectively, the adult's role in continuous provision is only to follow the lead of the child, interact when invited, and allow time and opportunity for the learners to interact with the resource in their own way.

Continuous provision of play in a classroom takes away the element of play being a treat or a reward. It also reassures students that learning through play is here to stay. The consistency of play's presence in your classroom allows your learners to relax into it, to trust that play is available to them when they need it, and not to rush to it in case it disappears. As mentioned before, when I tried to offer play as a finishing activity or a reward, it ended in disaster, with pupils rushing through their work, not completing it to their best, or even not attempting the work as they wanted to play. Keep the play available and consistent as part of your classroom and a part of your learning and teaching activities.

What follows are some ideas for continuous provision that you can set up in your classroom that will offer challenge to older learners as well as providing opportunity for creativity, exploration, and investigation.

Play Trays

Space is a bit of a luxury in an upper stages classroom, so having a range of contextual areas and tables with activities available might not seem very feasible. What I have found useful is discovering tray units that hold boxes and trays of different sizes or cube units with canvas boxes. These trays or boxes can be as few or as many as you can manage without giving up too much floor space or storage!

Each year, I provide my class with some trays already filled and some empty trays for them to suggest resources for. Your trays or boxes could contain any of the suggested resources from Chapter 8, such as small world characters, cars, art activities, or home corner resources. Get to know your class, ask them what they are interested in and what they would like to play with. You may end up with trays full of dressing-up clothes and dolls or simply Uno cards and fidget toys. The important thing is that it comes from your learners; otherwise, they won't have any interest in playing with them.

Continuous Provision

I have had a wide range of themes in my Play Trays over the years, but here are some examples. I like to label them as stuff, as it leaves things a bit open-ended and invites some adaptation and imagination.

Science Stuff	Car Stuff	Puzzle Stuff	Calm Stuff
Home Stuff	Fashion Stuff	Challenge Stuff	Building Stuff
Arty Stuff	Colouring Stuff	Office Stuff	Crafty Stuff
Magnifying Stuff	Circuit Stuff	Balancing Stuff	Magnetic Stuff

It's a good idea to tailor the trays or boxes to meet the interests and needs of your class as much as you can, but also to include some resources that might guide their learning in a way that links to the themes you are teaching. During a period of teaching measure, I try to have tape measures, rulers, metre sticks, and a long retractable tape measure for the class to access. Inevitably, there will be some learners who want to measure how tall they are, how wide the classroom is, or how big their handspan is – and the independent exploration of this is what deepens their understanding of measure.

If you don't have space for a tray unit, a few stackable boxes with lids or tubs you can keep under a desk will work just as well. As long as the students know where they are and are able to access them independently, how you store them is irrelevant really.

Tuff Trays

Tuff Trays are a great way to provide an element of continuous provision in your classroom. How you use them will depend on your learning environment, your learners, and you as a

Figure 16.1 Play Trays

teacher. Tuff Trays come in various sizes, so depending on your available space, you may opt for a large one on a stand, or you can select something smaller that can sit on a table, beside a sink, or even on a windowsill.

You may wish to have it available on a timetabling basis – every child gets allotted time to access the tray if they wish. I recommend not having it as a compulsory task but as an option that students can access at appropriate times. Alternatively, you can have it as an activity for those who need some time to get ready for learning, have finished a given task, or need a break from learning. I have it available at a range of times – for those struggling to engage for a reason and needing a brain break, as a finishing option, or as a Friday afternoon brain game.

However you decide to use it, a Tuff Tray should have a purpose for your learners. And contain an activity that is age and stage-appropriate for your class. Here are some ideas for activities that can challenge and engage older learners.

Construction

Construction challenges can engage, develop fine motor skills, and create an opportunity for some physical manipulation of materials to solve a problem. Allow freedom to create. Many Tuff Trays contain a specific challenge – Can you build a house for the toy family? How tall a tower can you build? – but if you are leaving a challenge like this out for older learners, be mindful of limiting their creativity. Instead of asking learners to "build a house", perhaps "create somewhere for the family to live" would produce more of a range of results – houses, motor homes, tents!

Providing a range of materials to build with also offers opportunities for logistical thinking. Junk modelling, Lego, wooden blocks, Kapla, and so on are all great for learners to get stuck into and see what they can create. And don't be afraid to mix materials and leave a selection for them to choose the most appropriate for their construction. It's not for us to decide what will work for them, but for them to discover for themselves.

Creative Thinking

Have some materials left out on the tray, and just let your class be creative.

Some children can find this quite overwhelming. Much like being faced with a blank page, the idea of coming up with something from scratch with absolutely no guidance whatsoever can leave them blank, baffled, and overwhelmed. If your learners find it quite tricky to come up with their own ideas, particularly if this level of autonomy is fairly new to them, give them some questions to help them out:

What can you build with these materials?
What kind of a job might use these materials?
What is the tallest structure you can create?
Create a sculpture to represent your favourite song/hobby/sport/celebrity.

You could also help inspire them by leaving some pictures on the tray alongside the materials. Pictures of sculptures, buildings, or early inventions might help them come up with their own ideas.

The important thing is not to create the impression that there are right or wrong options at this station. Anything the learners create is correct. Encourage them to describe their creations and explain their thinking behind them.

Themed:

Valentine's Day – Some blank cards, red and pink tissue paper, and some poetry inspiration.
Christmas – Wrapping paper, Sellotape, gift bags, and blank cards.
Easter – Egg templates, stamps, stencils, and blank cards.
Holidays – Travel brochures, hotel websites, play money (different currencies if possible).

Link your Tuff Tray resources to your current learning, if possible. For an activity to be considered play, try not to direct the learners specifically; let them use their imagination and creativity. You can, however, support and encourage their learning around a certain theme by providing certain materials and resources. Leave out some of these resources and see what your learners do with them. If you feel they need more structure or guidance, pose some vague, open-ended questions. Just don't expect specific answers, and certainly don't mark their responses. Simply give them feedback, ask about how they found out, and wonder about what else they might discover.

Here are some examples of tuff tray themes with suggested materials and questions that might provoke targeted upper stages learning.

Learning Theme	Resources/Materials	Questions
Measure	Tape measures, rulers, stacking/linking blocks	How long? How far? How tall?
Properties of Matter	Chalk, rock, sand, water, coffee powder	How does it feel? How hard? How soft? Does it mix?
Time	Clock, egg timers, stopwatch, train or bus timetables	How fast? How long? What time? Which bus/train?
Spelling	Scrabble tiles, magnetic letters, letter stencils	How do you spell? Which sounds can be made in different ways?
Chance	Dice, Deck of cards	What are the chances? How many rolls before you get a _____? How many cards before you get a _____?

Thinking Skills

Riddles

In the next section, there is a selection of thinking skills, including riddles designed to elicit problem-solving and out-of-the-box thinking. These riddles can be written onto the Tuff Tray with a chalk pen (or similar) or displayed on a board with some props and some time provided for exploration and investigation.

134 *Practical Lesson Ideas*

The Farmer

Resources: 3 Items to represent a dog, goat, and cabbage (Duplo is great for this!)
Learning Area: Problem-solving
Activity: A farmer has a dog, a goat, and a cabbage. He must get himself and all three across the river, but his boat will only hold him and one other. If left alone, the dog will bite the goat, and the goat will eat the cabbage. How can he get everyone across safely?
Solution: The farmer brings the goat across first and leaves it on the other side. He returns for the cabbage (or dog, it doesn't matter which) and brings it across. He returns with the goat. He then picks up the dog (or cabbage) and brings it across, finally returning for the goat.
There are variations of this riddle involving a fox, chicken and grain, or a wolf, rabbit, and lettuce, etc., but you get the idea, and you can substitute any three creatures (or people!) you like.

Figure 16.2 Farmer Riddle

Paper Cutting

Resources: A4 Paper (this can be from your scrap paper tray as the pupils are just going to cut it up!)
Learning Area: Measure, Mathematical Thinking, Logic
Activity: How can you cut a single sheet of A4 paper so that you can fit yourself through a hole in the middle?

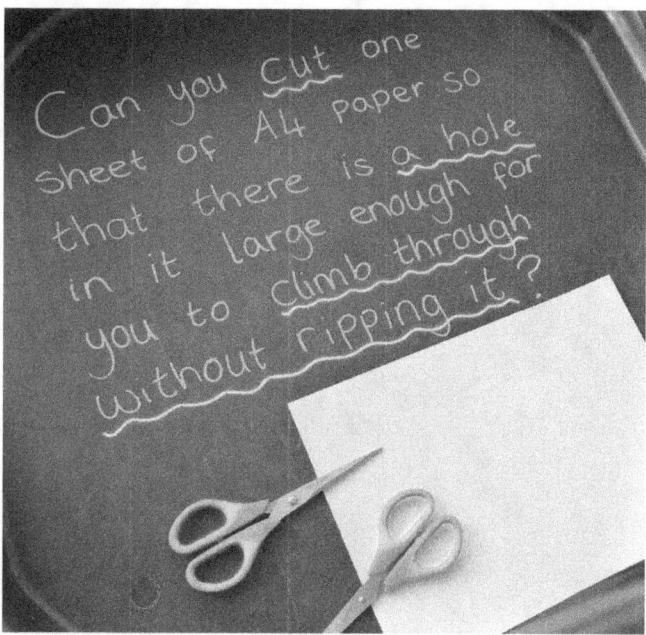

Figure 16.3 Paper Cutting

(Continued)

136 *Practical Lesson Ideas*

(Continued)

Solution: It turns out that there are primary-aged children who can fit through a rectangle cut in the middle of a sheet of paper, so if your learners are on the smaller side, I would change the wording of the problem to request a hole that their teacher can fit through!
Fold the paper in half and cut as shown.
Open the paper out and cut the central sections, leaving the outer edge intact.
You should now have a huge hole, big enough to step through.

Figure 16.3a–c Paper Cutting Solution

(Continued)

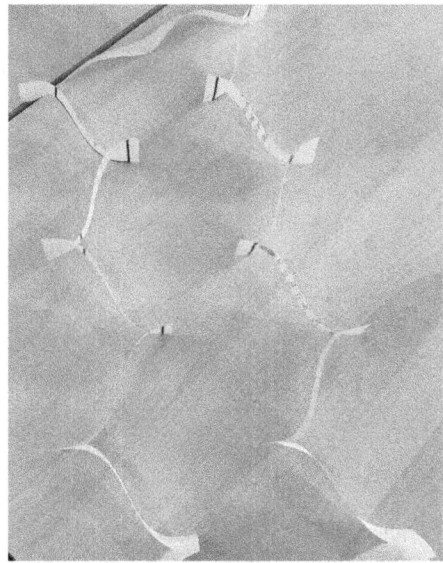

Figure 16.3a–c Continued

Measuring Jugs

Also known as the 'Riddle from Die Hard'.

Resources:	Jugs or cups to represent 5L and 3L (or 500ml and 300ml) jugs and an empty jug or bowl
Learning Area:	Measure, Mathematical Thinking, Logic
Activity:	I need 4L of water, but I only have a 5L jug and a 3L jug. How can I use the jugs I have to accurately measure out 4L?
	I like to provide two measuring cups of different sizes to represent the jugs and an empty container, but you can be more precise with 300ml and 500ml containers or 30ml and 50ml scoops if you have them and if your learners are comfortable working with these numbers.
Solution:	There are a few solutions to this problem that will give you 4L – and if you are lucky, a child will come up with a new solution altogether!
	Fill the 5L jug, then use this to fill the 3L jug. This leaves 2L in the 5L jug. Pour this into the empty container, and then repeat.
	Alternatively, Fill the 3L jug and pour it into the empty container. Repeat twice more to give 9L in the empty container. Then, use the 5L jug to remove water, leaving 4L.
	Or, fill the 3L jug and pour it into the 5L jug. Repeat, as this will leave 1L in the 3L jug. Pour this into the empty container. Now, use the 3L jug to top up to 4L.

138 *Practical Lesson Ideas*

Money Problem

Resources:	None – but it might help to have some play money available so learners can act out the problem and work backwards.
Learning Area:	Measure, Mathematical Thinking, Problem-Solving
Activity:	A man spent three-quarters of his money and then lost three-quarters of the money he had left. He has £6 (or $6 or €6) left. How much money did he have to start with?
Solution:	He had £96 (or $96 or €96). He spent ¾ of it (£72). He lost ¾ of the remaining £24 (£18). So he was left with £6. You can adapt this problem in any way you like by changing the amounts of money and the fractions. A much simpler riddle could be something like: A man spent half of his money in a shop. He now has £10. How much did he have to start with?

Sailing Weight Limits

Resources:	Dolls or characters to represent the four people in the riddle, a boat, and a small bag (or items to represent them)
Learning Area:	Measure, Mathematical Thinking, Logic
Activity:	This riddle is similar to The Farmer but with a bit more numeracy involved! Mary, Jim, Sam, and Jo (or any four names you like) need to cross the river. The boat can hold 80kg. Mary is 60kg, Jim is 70kg, Sam is 40kg, and Jo is 30kg. They also have 20kg of supplies. How can they all get across the river using the boat?
Solution:	There are various ways to solve this, but they all hinge on Sam and Jo bringing the boat back to pick up the next load.

Figure 16.4 River Crossing Riddle

(Continued)

An example of a solution is: • Jo and Sam cross • Sam comes back • Jim crosses • Jo comes back • Jo and Sam cross • Jo comes back • Mary and the supplies cross • Sam comes back • Finally, Jo and Sam cross This can be modified by changing the names and the values of the weights as well as the boat limit. You can add an extra challenge with tricker numbers or adapt it for support with easier numbers.

Essentially, your continuous provision needs to be provided continuously! If you only have space for some boxes, then keep those boxes for at least a term before you change them too much. If you have a tuff tray, keep it out all year, changing the activities on it as you need to. Don't put these resources away to make room for something else or remove them because work hasn't been completed or behaviour isn't to your liking. Find other consequences, such as limiting time with the resources or who they can play with but keep the resources there – consistency is key.

17 Concluding Thoughts

Whichever way you choose to bring play into your classroom, it's worth remembering to have fun with it, but keep focussing on the skills the learners are developing. As our learners prepare for their next steps through education and into the wider world, play can offer a great way to prepare for further education, work, and the life skills they will need. However, we should also prepare them for a stage of education where there might not be much opportunity to play, but they will be required to work independently, work with others, motivate themselves, and drive themselves to succeed. As learners prepare to move on to the next stage of their education, they will also need to be ready to follow instructions, to complete tasks to a deadline, and to complete specific given tasks. It may seem like these skills fly directly in the face of the play principles I have previously outlined. And they do, to a certain extent, but that is why I have emphasised a balance of teacher-led and child-led approaches.

The opportunities to apply learning in a contextualised capacity can sit alongside some of these other aspects as you introduce boundaries, challenges, and rules. Add to your play activities by setting time limits, rules about the materials used, or people you work with they can work with. Add success criteria so they have a target to aim for or a challenge that helps them understand whether their work has met its purpose. This leads to self-evaluation and reflection within the parameters of the play principles – self-motivation, personally driven, and freely chosen.

Create a culture of questioning, personal growth, encouragement, and, most of all, an environment where it is safe to try out things to see what works for you. We all know that we learn from our mistakes, but we also learn from our successes. If learners feel comfortable enquiring and questioning, they will engage in their learning in order to find out the answers.

> Look for playful moments throughout your day.
> Give your learners time, space, and opportunities to explore and investigate.
> Don't be afraid to make mistakes.
> Don't be afraid to make a mess.
> Remember, playfulness is fun!

Take what you need from this book to support you on your journey. Feel free to dip in and out of it, take lesson ideas, and tweak them to suit your own situation. Use them as starting points to develop your whole play approach.

DOI: 10.4324/9781003486602-21

I would love to hear how you all get on – shared ideas and resources only help us become better teachers and educators. We are a community, and I look forward to hearing how some of you get on with your own play adventures.

Find me on Instagram, Threads, or X (formerly Twitter): @mrs_s_learns

Useful Websites and Links

UNCRC - www.unicef.org.uk/

International Play Association - https://ipaworld.org/

National Institute for Play - https://nifplay.org/

International Day of Play - www.internationaldayofplay.org/

United Kingdom

Scotland

Play Scotland - www.playscotland.org/
Scottish Government, (2013) Play Strategy for Scotland: Our Vision, Edinburgh: Scottish Government www.gov.scot/publications/play-strategy-scotland-vision/

England

Play England - www.playengland.org.uk/

Wales

Play Wales/Chwarae Cymru - https://play.wales/

Northern Ireland

Playboard NI - www.playboard.org/

Australia

Play Australia - www.playaustralia.org.au/

Australian Children's Education and Care Authority (2024), *The Importance of Play in Children's Learning and Development* Retrieved from www.startingblocks.gov.au/resources/children-and-services/educational-programs/the-importance-of-play-in-childrens-learning-and-development

Canada

Outdoor Play Canada - www.outdoorplaycanada.ca/
Right to Play - https://righttoplay.ca/en/

United States of America

Play and Playground Encyclopedia (2019). *US Play Coalition* Retrieved from www.pgpedia.com/u/us-play-coalition

India

Government of India (2020), National Education Policy, Ministry of Human Resource Development. Retrieved from www.education.gov.in/sites/upload_files/mhrd/files/NEP_Final_English_0.pdf

Finland

Finnish National Agency for Education (2019) The Essence of Play. Retrieved from www.oph.fi/en/blog/essence-play

Appendix A: APDR and PDSA

APDR - Assess, Plan, Do, Review

Aim What is our main aim? What do we want to achieve?		Start Date	Target Group	Review Date
Assess	What data do we have, and what does it tell us?			
	What else do we need to find out?			
Plan	What is the intended outcome, and how will we measure it?			
	How do we plan to implement this change/intervention?			
Do	What happened during implementation?			
Review	What does this data tell us about the intervention?			
	What do we need to do next?			

PDSA - Plan, Do, Study, Act

	Aim Describe the test of change: What are we trying to accomplish?	By whom?	When?	Where?
P	Plan The tasks needed to set up this change	By whom?	When?	Where?
	Predict what will happen	Measures to determine if prediction succeeds		
D	DO Describe what happened when you ran the test			
S	STUDY Describe the measured results and how they compared to the prediction			
A	ACT Describe what needs to happen next			

Appendix B: Timetable

	Monday	Tuesday	Wednesday	Thursday	Friday
Morning Challenge	Handwriting activity	Spelling activity	Riddle	Quiet reading	Mini challenge
Period 1	Numeracy - Textbooks	Numeracy - word problems/ context	Assembly Numeracy - online quiz	Maths/Numeracy - STEM challenge (linked to Numeracy focus)	Numeracy - Stations or games
Break					
Period 2	Writing - tools for writing Spelling activity (workbooks) Novel Study task	Writing - tools for writing & grammar Spelling activity (workbooks) Novel Study task	Writing - tools for writing Reading Comprehension quiz	Writing - themed to topic. Link to grammar and writing tools lessons Listening and Talking activity	Spelling test Free Write Friday Weekly Quiz (general knowledge with occasional curricular question)
Lunch					
Period 3	Interdisciplinary Learning (Topic work) Information sharing, gathering, or research	Technologies - coding, short film making, spreadsheet work, etc.	Health and Wellbeing - real-life situations, role-play, discussions, etc. Together 21 time	Interdisciplinary Learning (Topic work) Using information from Mon to create something new	PE - Small-sided game play
Period 4	RE - following school programme	PE - Independent and paired skills	Maths - Practical activities following a short textbook	RE - following school programme (link to Ex. Arts)	Independent Learning

Appendix C: Construction Materials

Resources	Wooden Blocks Duplo K*Nex	Lego Kapla Junk	Magnetic Squares
Potential Challenges/ Questions	Design and build a house for a hamster. What could you create using the materials provided? Build a house that is half as wide as it is tall. Provide pictures of famous buildings to copy. Design a solution to our messy classroom. STEM challenge cards – rafts, boats, kites, bridges, etc. With a base area of 900cm², what can you create?		
Meta Skills	**Focusing** • Attention • Filtering **Adapting** • Openness • Critical reflection • Adaptability • Self-learning • Resilience **Initiative** • Independent thinking • Decision-making • Self-motivation **Collaborating** • Teamworking and collaboration **Leading** • Inspiring others	**Curiosity** • Problem recognition **Creativity** • Imagination • Idea generation • Visualising • Maker mentality **Sense-Making** • Holistic thinking • Synthesis • Analysis **Critical Thinking** • Deconstruction • Logical thinking • Computational thinking	

(Continued)

(Continued)

Experiences and Outcomes	I can extend and enhance my design skills to solve problems and construct models. TCH 2-09 I can recognise basic properties and uses for a variety of materials and can discuss which ones are most suitable for a given task. TCH 2-10a I can use a range of graphic techniques, manually and digitally, to communicate ideas, concepts, or products, experimenting with the use of shape, colour, and texture to enhance my work. TCH 2-11a I can extend my knowledge and understanding of engineering disciplines to create solution. TCH 2-12a I can use my knowledge of the sizes of familiar objects or places to assist me when making an estimate of measure. MNU 2-11a I can explain how different methods can be used to find the perimeter and area of a simple 2D shape or volume of a simple 3D object. MNU 2-11c

Index

Note: Page numbers in *italics* indicate figures, and page numbers in **bold** indicate tables in the text

action research 43
adult-led playful learning *see* playful learning
alphabet stories 87
American Academy of Pediatrics (AAP) Clinical Reports 12
angles classification 81
angles in action 80
Around the World 75-76
art 55, 62, 118-119
Assess, Plan, Do, Review (APDR) 41, 43, 125, 144
attainment-related targets 32-33
Attainment Scale 42, 43, **43**
attention to detail 119

back-to-back game 76-77
balance and coordination 110-111; balance cards 111; dice balance 111
balance cards 111
ball carry 110
ball skills 107; benchball 108; Dodgeball/soft balls 108
barriers and solutions 32-37; attainment-related targets 32-33; behaviour management 36; resistance to new initiatives 33; teaching curriculum 34-35; workload 35-36
beach fun 76
behaviour management 36
benchball 108
binary coding 77
bingo 69-70, *70*
blankety-blank 88-89
board games 112, 123, 128
boats-sailing/rafts 97, *97*

book club 94
Buckley, H.E. 120
Burns, M. 15

cable cars 98
cafe 129
chain reactions 103
child-led play *see* free play
class economy 128
class garden 126
classroom: cleaning resources *48*; layout 47; no one-size-fits-all approach to play 58; numeracy resources 49-50, *51*; organisation 47; pedagogy 58-60; reading resources 49, *50*; recommended resources for **52**; resourcing play 52-56; seating choice 48-49; timetable opportunities for play 59-60; *see also* specific entries
conceptual learning 14, 59
A Connect 4 (4-in-a-Row) game 89
Consequences game 87
construction 54, 132, 147-148
contextual learning 21-25, 58-59; opportunities 63-65, 140
continuous provision 27, 59, 130; in classroom 47; construction challenges 132; creative thinking 132-133; farmer riddle 133-134, *134*; money problem 138; paper cutting 135-136, *135-136*; Play Trays 130-131, *131*; Riddle from Die Hard 137; river crossing riddle *138*; sailing weight limits 138-139; thinking skills 133-138; Tuff Trays 131-132
Convention on the Rights of the Child 5
coordination *see* balance and coordination
coronavirus pandemic 13, 22

Index

creative play 7
creative thinking 132-133
Curriculum for Excellence (CfE) 9

Danniels, E. 6
darts dice 72-73, *73*
deal or no deal 82
dice balance 111
dice game 55
digital technologies 121-122
discount card 79-80
Dodgeball/soft balls 108
Dominoes Cards 89-90
Duplo characters 53

early years, play: benefits 12-16; classroom 53; observations 40; *vs.* upper stages 19-20
earthquake simulation 99
educational policy, play 9-10
egg drop challenge 98-99
emotional health and wellbeing 114-116; expressionism 114; quiet time 115-116; story time 115; talking time 114-115
Engagement Scale 42, **42**
enriched curriculum 9
escape room 122
expressionism 114, 120

farmer riddle 133-134, *134*
fashion show 129
Field, J.: *Oi Frog* 15
fine motor skills 7
Fleer, M. 6
floor book 39-40
Floor is Lava 109-110
follow directions 81
formal observations 40
Fosbury, D. 62-63
freely chosen 28-29
free play 6, 27, 57; opportunities 19
free writing 60
full-on play 58

games: listening and talking 83; with rules 7; show 122; *see also* specific games
Getting it Right for Every Child (GIRFEC) 9
get to know each other 84-85
Ginsburg, K.R. 6

Gray, K.: *Oi Frog* 15
Gray, P. 6
greater than or less than 74-75, *75*
Griffiths, A. 15
gross motor skills 7
Guess Who 55
guided play 6-7
Guinness Book of Records 93

Headbandz 55
health and wellbeing 107-116; balance and coordination 110-111; balance cards 111; ball carry 110; ball skills 107; benchball 108; board games 112; dice balance 111; Dodgeball/soft balls 108; emotional 114-116; expressionism 114; Floor is Lava 109-110; hoop pass 110; netball game 109; new partners 112-113; no instructions 113; physical education 107; quiet time 115-116; social 112-113; story time 115; talking time 114-115; teamwork 109-110; use balloons 107-108
His Majesty's Inspectorate of Education (HMIe) 42
Home Seats 49
hoop pass 110
hybrid model of play pedagogy 7

imaginative play 7, 120
inclusive learning 13
independent learning 16, 62, 63
independent talks/presentations 85
informal observations 40
intrinsic motivation 29-30
inventors 105
I Spy 83

Jeopardy! 70-71

kites 96

land formation 117-118
learning environment 62, 65; learners ownership 16; and physical activity 9-10, 62-63; supportive and quality 30
Lego 112; park design 126-127, *127*
letter tiles 60
Leuven 5-point Scale 41, **42**
literacy 83-94
Loop Cards 89-90

marble mazes 103
marble ramps 103-104, *104*
matching activities 123
McGuinness, C. 13
McKendrick, J. 6
Messy Maths 22
Meta Skills Progression Framework 40
Minister's Cat 84
money problem 138
moral education 121
movement 9-10, 12
musical chairs 49

national play organisations, Scotland 9
new partners 112-113
no instructions 113
non-negotiable tasks 58-59
nonsense sentences 86
number relay 78
numeracy 59, 61-62; angles classification 81; angles in action 80; Around the World 75-76; back-to-back 76-77; beach fun 76; binary coding 77; bingo 69-70, *70*; darts dice 72-73, *73*; deal or no deal 82; discounts card 79-80; estimating metre 82; follow the directions 81; greater than or less than 74-75, *75*; Jeopardy! 70-71; and mathematics 69-82; noughts and crosses 77; number relay 78; plan a journey 78; resources *51*; Simon Says 80; speeds calculation 79; target slide 73-74, *74*; tic-tac-toe 77; Uno cards 71-72, *72*; word problems in 23-24
nurturing relationships, play 12

observations, play 40
Oi Frog (Gray and Field) 15
older years *see* upper years, play
openers cubes 87
outdoor learning 49

paper cutting 135-136, *135-136*
parachute 98
park design 126-127, *127*
personally driven 30-31
personal relevance 16
Peterson, A. 6
physical activity 9-10, 12
physical education 107

Piaget's concrete operational stage 19
place value dice *20*
Plan, Do, Study, Act (PDSA) 41, 43, 145
planned interventions 41-42
play 5-10; and academic achievement 20; advocating benefits of 9; barriers and solutions 32-37; categories of 7; challenge 20-21; definitions 5; development of 9; element of 16; levels 6-8; opportunity and experience 12-13; perceptions of learning and 58-59; principles 140; rules and boundaries 7; as tool for engagement and attainment 9; types of 7-8; *see also* specific entries
play-based curriculum 13, 19
play-based learning 6-7, 27, 57; benefits 12-17; beyond early years 21-22; debate 14; development of 9; ethos 15; intervention 38; measurement of impact 38
Play-Doh 65
playful learning 7-8, 13-14, 57; activities 122-123; ethos 15, 57-66; flexibility and 15; reading activity 93-94
Play Trays 130-131, *131*
pollution/energy waste 127
principles of play 5-6, 13, 15, 27, 117; freely chosen 28-29; intrinsic motivation 29-30; personally driven 30-31
Progress Review of Scotland's Play Strategy 9
project-based learning 124-130
pulleys/cable cars 98
pupil feedback 41
pupil records 41
Pyle, A. 6

quiet time 115-116
quizzes 122

reading 93-94; enjoyment of 61; for information 61
record keeping 38-43, 65
record of work 39; pupil records 41; reflection book *39*, 39-40
reflection book *39*, 39-40
regular play 57
religious education 121
resistance to new initiatives 33

152 Index

resourcing play, in classroom 52–56; construction 54; creative and artistic opportunities 55; dice game 55; Guess Who 55; Headbandz 55; role play 53; small world manipulation 52–53; toy cars 54, *54*; Uno cards 55–56, *56*
Riddle from Die Hard 137
Right to Play 9
river crossing riddle *138*
role-playing 21, 24, 53, 120

sailing weight limits 138–139
scale models 102, *102*
Science, Technology, Engineering, Arts, and Mathematics (STEM) 6, 59, 95–106; boats-sailing/rafts 97, *97*; bridges 100, *100*; chain reactions 103; earthquake simulation 99; egg drop challenge 98–99; inventors 105; kites 96; marble mazes 103; marble ramps 103–104, *104*; mixtures and reactions 101; parachute 98; pulleys/cable cars 98; scale models 102, *102*; water cycle 104–105; waterways 101; withstand flood 99–100; zip wires 96–97
Scotland's Play Strategy 9
self-publishing 129
sequences 123
Shopping Game 84
shopping role-play 21, 24, *24*
Simon Says 80
Simpson Attainment Scale 43, **43**
Simpson Engagement Scale 42, **42**
skills developement, through play 12–14
small world manipulation 52–53
Smart Play Network 9
social health and wellbeing 112–113; board games 112; new partners 112–113; no instructions 113
social play 8
solution-focussed approach 32, 36; *see also* barriers and solutions
speeds calculation 79
spelling: activities 92; stations 92–93; teacher 92

story time 115
styles of painting 119

talking time 114–115
target slide 73–74, *74*
teaching curriculum 34–35
teamwork activity 109–110; ball carry 110; Floor is Lava 109–110; hoop pass 110
10-word stories 86
theoretical learning 59
thinking skills: farmer riddle 133–134, *134*; money problem 138; paper cutting 135–136, *135–136*; Riddle from Die Hard 137; river crossing riddle *138*; sailing weight limits 138–139
tic-tac-toe 77
timetable 59–60, 146
toy cars 54, *54*
traditional learning 33; project-based learning *vs.* 124
trauma recovery, play and 13, 22
true play 6, 20
Tuff Tray 22, 41, 47, 49, 131–132; challenge 132; themes 133

Uno cards 55–56, *56*, 71–72, *72*
upper years, play 22–23, 25; early years *vs.* 19–20; reading resources 49, *50*; Tuff Tray themes 133

Wallace, W. 120
water cycle 65, 104–105
waterways 101
weather 118
wellbeing *see* emotional health and wellbeing; health and wellbeing; social health and wellbeing
withstand flood, STEM 99–100
word problems, in numeracy 23–24, 59, 62
workload 35–36
writing: free 60; playful 85–86; provocations 90–91; tools for 91

zip wires 96–97

For Product Safety Concerns and Information please contact our EU
representative GPSR@taylorandfrancis.com
Taylor & Francis Verlag GmbH, Kaufingerstraße 24, 80331 München, Germany